IMMIGRANT LABOUR IN KUWAIT

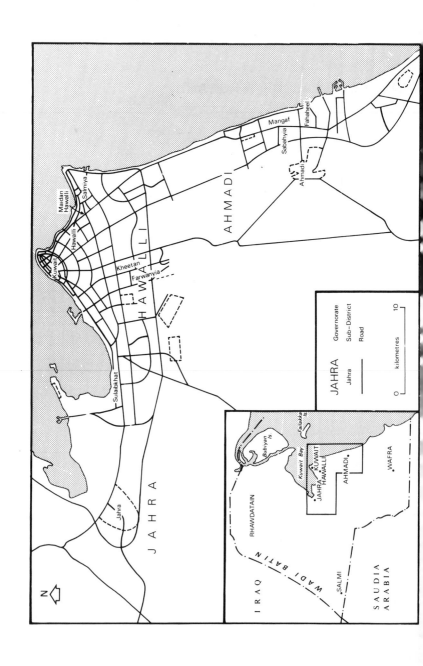

Immigrant Labour in KUWAIT

ABDULRASOOL AL-MOOSA
and KEITH McLACHLAN

CROOM HELM
London ● Sydney ● Dover, New Hampshire

© 1985 A. A. Al-Moosa and K. S. McLachlan
Croom Helm Ltd, Provident House, Burrell Row,
Beckenham, Kent BR3 1AT

Croom Helm Australia Pty Ltd, First Floor,
139 King Street, Sydney, NSW 2001, Australia

British Library Cataloguing in Publication Data

Al-Moosa, Abdulrasool
   Immigrant labour in Kuwait.
   1. Alien labour—Kuwait
   I. Title   II. McLachlan, K. S.
   331.6'2'095367   HD8669

   ISBN 0-7099-3554-4

Croom Helm, 51 Washington Street,
Dover, New Hampshire 03820, USA

Library of Congress Cataloging in Publication Data

Musa, 'Abd Al-Rasul 'ALI.
   Immigrant Labour in Kuwait

   Includes Index.
   1. Alien Labor — Kuwait. I. McLachlan, K.S.
(Kieth Stanley) II. Title
HD8669.M87   1984   331.6'2'095367   84-29316
ISBN 0-7099-3554-4

Printed and bound in Great Britain by
Biddles Ltd, Guildford and King's Lynn

CONTENTS

TABLES

FIGURES

ACKNOWLEDGEMENTS

This study was based on a long period of preparation and work in the field. The authors wish to acknowledge the many organisations and individuals who have given assistance at all stages of the research programme. Special mention must be made of the parts played by Ali Abdulla, Mahmud Assayed, Nabil Jar Jes, Kheder Kabandi, Dr Ahmad Khalifa, Osman Mirgani, Dr Farouk Shalabi, Dr Mostafa Shalagani, Gladys Stevens and Dr Mohammed Taleb.

The University of Kuwait was generous throughout in its encouragement of the research and thanks are offered to the officers of the University and to those of the staff of the Geography Department who took an active and positive interest in the project.

Funding for the fieldwork programmes in Kuwait and Egypt, together with computer processing of data gathered and essential travel by members of the research team, was provided by the Kuwait Foundation for the Advancement of Sciences. The strong backing given by the Foundation to the project is gratefully acknowledged by the authors.

Among the many institutions outside Kuwait that deserve thanks are the School of Oriental and African Studies, London University, and the National Centre for Social and Crime Research in Egypt.

1   INTRODUCTION

Thanks to the generosity of the Kuwait Foundation for the Advancement of Sciences and the University of Kuwait, the authors undertook a field study of the social and economic aspects of the domestic and foreign labour force and their impact on the State, beginning in 1980.

The terms of reference set at the inception specified that the study would look in depth at the costs and benefits of the existence of a large foreign labour force in Kuwait, this within the framework of the general problem of labour demand and supply within the State. It was hoped that the research would enable more light to be thrown on the nature of the foreign labour force than was previously possible and that illumination would remove the prejudices and misconceptions surrounding its presence in Kuwait.

At the start of the research, a number of basic questions were posed concerned with the foreign labour force for which it was expected the study would provide answers. These six main enquiries were:

1. The structure of the non-Kuwaiti labour force.
2. Social factors bearing on the foreign workforce.
3. Economic factors bearing on the foreign workforce.
4. Interactions between the Kuwaiti and non-Kuwaiti workforces.
5. The implications for social and economic planning in Kuwait of the particular foreign communities that comprised the non-Kuwaiti workforce.
6. Likely effects of income remittance and skill transfers on the countries of origin of migrant workers.

Whereas data have been collected by a variety of official sources on the structure of the foreign workforce, their coverage has been generally limited. This study set out, therefore, to examine eight factors deemed to be relevant to elaboration of the structure of employment of foreign groups in Kuwait. Items included in the survey were the country of origin, length of stay, educational status, age structure, geographical distribution in Kuwait, past employment, occupation in Kuwait and all other appropriate materials. Much of the material gathered on the structure of the foreign labour force was designed to permit comparison with surveys of the labour force in Kuwait as a whole, to highlight changes over time and the degree to which the foreign labour force deviated from the mean. Analysis of the structure of the foreign workforce also enabled the context to be set against which detailed examination of the economic and social factors working within this arena could be placed.

Among the main objectives of this research project was the creation of a bank of data on social factors at work within the foreign communities that provide the basic workforce in Kuwait. It was above all designed to show the special characteristics of each group by national origin *inter alia* as they affected the efficiency of the foreign workforce as a whole. Areas attracting attention were the location of workers in Kuwait, levels of education, housing problems and other factors aiding or inhibiting effective participation of foreign groups in the Kuwaiti labour force.

Parallel with the above study, and of equal weight, a review of the economic aspects of the foreign communities was undertaken. It was felt that detailed information was required on matters such as wage levels for individuals and households together with effects of multiple employment. This section, too, looked at how far the foreign labour force brought in appropriate skills to Kuwait and used them in their employment there. The costs to Kuwait of the foreign workforce as measured by the out-flow of funds and other calls on Kuwaiti resources were to be established within an overall assessment of the foreign contribution to the Kuwaiti economy.

Given a large foreign labour force in Kuwait, by all estimates larger by far than the indigenous workforce, it had to be asked how far the foreign and local labour inter-react by way of skill transfers, co-operation or competition. The separation of the two groups by sectors of employment or on social grounds was looked at, as were relative costs to the economy of the two.

Implicit in the research were other lines of enquiry which were not necessarily itemised within the specific data-gathering systems. It was, for example, recognized that the unbalanced nature of the workforce in Kuwait presented very special planning problems. When the characteristics of each foreign community are taken into account as well as the absolute size of the foreign origin input, and when there might be local and international political factors to consider when ensuring the welfare of the foreign workforce, it appears that there is not so absolute a freedom of choice for the planners as would at first appear in a wealthy oil-exporting state. The survey was designed to help discussion of the planning problem by setting reliable statistical limits to some of the hitherto unquantified elements of the matter.

In recognition of the fact that the ultimate objective of this survey was the foreign labour force and that overseas workers came to Kuwait primarily with the aim of remitting as high a level of income as feasible to their countries of origin, it was decided that there would be an attempt to assess the effects of remittances from Kuwait on a select sample of the foreign workforce. It was proposed that information be gathered in the home towns and villages of this sample to see whether or not there was a positive impact of remittances at the individual, family or local community levels. Such studies could at best be tentative but would at least suggest ways in which action in Kuwait might ease problems generated by the remittances to poorer societies, especially those of the Arab world.

The terms of reference established at the beginning of the study proved to be largely apposite. Problems under review became more pressing from an economic and political point of view as work progressed. By April 1982, the Kuwaiti authorities were calling for joint action by the Arab states of the Gulf area to control the growth of the foreign labour force.[1] Flows of foreign exchange from Kuwait in the form of remittances were running at a high level by 1981 at the same time that claims on Kuwaiti financial resources for domestic and other needs were rising rapidly while oil income was declining. Political instabilities in the Middle East outside Kuwait added to already existing feelings of unease among the indigenous community concerning so large a foreign workforce of unknown sympathies and loyalties. In effect, one of the key objectives of the enquiry of the survey — national origins of immigrant labour — had become a dominant matter of Kuwaiti concern by 1982, enhancing the utility of the survey and confirming the earlier judgement of the authors that this area was of critical interest (Al-Moosa and McLachlan 1980).

The discussion that follows is based above all on the results, both statistical and descriptive, of the field surveys implemented in Kuwait and Egypt by Dr A. A. Al-Moosa. An attempt is made to present the findings of the survey and their analysis in the form of five principal sections concerned, respectively, with the structure of the immigrant labour force, social factors bearing on the foreign working groups, the economic contribution of the immigrants to the State, the comparative status of the non-Kuwaitis against nationals with special reference to the costs and benefits of the former, and the likely outcome for the future of a continuation of present policies towards foreign labour.

There has been a conscious effort made to eschew an approach designed to appease either Kuwaiti or immigrant opinion. Wherever feasible, the authors have chosen to use the findings of their survey in preference to official data as a means of retaining as much freedom of attitude as was consistent with accuracy. The terms of reference of the original study required the authors to essay an estimate of the comparative costs and benefits arising from the presence of the immigrant workers and their families (bearing in mind that the survey was exclusively concerned with accompanied workers). Tools adopted to achieve these objectives will not find universal favour since they are manufactured *in situ* to suit the availabilities of supply of information at the disposal of the authors. While in no way claiming that the methodologies adopted are ideal, it might be suggested that they offer a first step out of the existing situation in which either entirely inappropriate alien models have been misapplied to Kuwait or qualitative judgements made from Olympian heights.

In many ways the findings of the survey confirm the deep problems that affect the foreign workforce in Kuwait and which, equally, adversely bear on the Kuwaitis themselves. It is demonstrated that many of the accompanied long-term members of the immigrant workforce are insecure and poorly paid in occupations for which they are not normally trained. Their presence has, however, been instrumental in creating conditions in which the indigenous community has developed a skewed structure of employment with extremely low productivity associated both with sinecure postings with state agencies and with depressed participation rates in gainful employment. The recurring features of Kuwait, in which on the one hand reliance on the immigrant workers seems doomed to persist and on the other Kuwaitis appear to wish for instant release from dependence on their visitors, is a paradox that is explored in a variety of ways in this study. The authors have found a multitude of linkages that seem to make the two groups in Kuwait mutually interdependent and as many reasons why those binding shackles should be broken. The frustrating problem for the Government of Kuwait and for every Kuwaiti citizen is that the two arenas have separate existences which have become internally reinforcing. The growth of foreign labour as a proportion of the total in Kuwait has continued in parallel with the augmenting disillusion of the State with its failure to gain self-sufficiency in the provision of a workforce. The authors of this volume have more than others before them, been convinced that there are no easy answers to the Kuwaiti dilemma (Alessa 1981, Mabro 1983). Disposing of the foreign workers has been intractable for a variety of good economic and social reasons that are frequently reinforced by political constraints. Even attempts to substitute non-Arab contract labour as a means of ensuring rapid repatriation of immigrant workers has not been a success (Birks and Sinclair 1980). At the other extreme, proposals for the absorption of Arabs into the Kuwaiti citizen population, for long recommended as a means of solving the issue at a stroke (Kuwait Planning Board 1968), has never mobilised adequate support among Kuwaitis to be appealing as a solution (Farah, Al-Salem and Al-Salem 1983).

If this study succeeds in demonstrating to a degree the nature of the umbilical cords that link the indigenous population to the immigrant workforce it has itself spawned and explains, albeit in part only, where interdependence is mutually useful or disadvantageous, then it has made a small addition of a more objective kind to what has become an emotionally charged debate, often more damaging than helpful.

Note

1.   The Kuwaiti English-language newspaper *Arab Times* published a front page report on 24th April 1982 under the title 'Arabic papers warn against Asian workers'. The article claimed that the scale of the labour flow was 'often to the detriment of the region'. Rai Al Aam newspaper carried similar reviews in Arabic on 23rd April.

References

Alessa, S. Y., *The manpower problem in Kuwait*, London, 1981, pp. 106-11.
Al-Moosa, A. A., and McLachlan, K. S., *Proposal for a Study of the Distribution of Occupational Groups in Kuwait — A Study of Socio-economic Aspects of Domestic and Foreign Labour Forces and Their Impact on Kuwaiti Economy and Society*, Kuwait, April 1980.
Birks, J. S., and Sinclair, C. A., 'Economic and social implications of current development in the Arab Gulf: The oriental connection', in Niblock, Tim (ed.), *Social and Economic Development in the Arab Gulf*, London, 1980, pp. 135-60.
Farah, T., Al-Salem, F., and Al-Salem, M. K., 'Arab labour migration: Arab migrants in Kuwait', in Asad, T., and Owen, R. (eds), *The Middle East*, Sociology of 'Developing Societies' Series, London, 1983, p. 52.
Kuwait Planning Board, *The First Five-year Development Plan, 1967/68-1971/72*, Kuwait, 1968, pp. 161-2.
Mabro, R., 'Immigrant workers and patterns of economic development', paper presented to a Seminar on Foreign Labour Migration in Arab Gulf Countries, The Arab Planning Institute/Centre for Arab Unity Studies, Kuwait, January 1983, pp. 7-11.

2 STRUCTURE OF THE IMMIGRANT LABOUR FORCE

The immigrant labour force in Kuwait is characterized by a wide variety of nationalities, ethnic groups, cultures and educational and professional standards. The contribution made by these immigrants is outstanding in its variety (68 different nationalities), quantity (over 50 per cent of total manpower) and quality (covering every sector of the economy). The absence of labour immigration restrictions has allowed this variety and made possible a meaningful study of the structure of immigrant manpower.

2.1 Origins of the immigrants

According to the 1980 Census, Arab nationals constitute the majority of immigrant manpower with 72.5 per cent, while Asians, 25 per cent, followed by Europeans, Africans and Americans make up the residue. These figures are not due to regulation of immigration but are a logical result of historic, geographic and economic factors. The Arab immigrants came to meet a need in various sectors, particularly in government departments which required workers sharing common elements with the indigenous society such as language, culture and social traits. In the case of the Asians such as Iranians, Indians and Pakistanis historic and geographic factors played a major role in their immigration to Kuwait. The Europeans are mainly British playing an important role in oil exploration, production and exportation.

Unfortunately, the 1980 Census did not include as in previous years details of immigrants' nationalities which makes the field data in this research, here examined against the 1975 Census, very important.

According to the 1975 Census, Arab nationals constituted 70 per cent of the immigrant manpower, this figure being made up of Palestinians/Jordanians (22 per cent), Egyptians (13 per cent) and Iraqis (8.5 per cent). In the non-Arab category Asians came first including Iranians (13.7 per cent), Indians (10 per cent) and Pakistanis (5.2 per cent). According to the research sample, figures were Palestinians (45 per cent), Egyptians (24 per cent), other Arab nationals (20 per cent) and for the non-Arabs, Indians (5 per cent).

Initially, immigration was encouraged from countries which shared common characteristics with Kuwait, emphasis being placed on Arab integration and co-operation. Arab ministers in employment conferences in 1965 and 1975 attempted to conclude agreements of labour transfer between Kuwait and other Arab countries including Egypt and Tunisia, but without success. In fact, from 1975 Asian manpower, particularly from Korea and the Philippines, added a new element for consideration.

The amount and diversity of immigrant manpower is attributed to ineffective planning and training programmes for the local labour force. This inefficiency and inadequacy of the local workforce has prepared the ground for immigration into Kuwait from all over the world. The fact that Kuwait is a free market and that there have been giant development projects, particularly in the services, has encouraged immigration.

The influx of peoples of 68 different nationalities represents more than just a number, it represents a complex of factors which have a serious impact on a wide range of socio-economic issues which are reflected in the development process itself. It is possible to find on one work-site a number of people representing many different languages, cultures and traditions. Communication between such members of a group is difficult and this is shown in the low work quality and the slow pace of production. Communication problems are not confined to the immigrant community but affect the local workers who must organise and administrate foreign labour at all levels.

2.2   Period of residence in Kuwait

The period of residence of immigrant manpower in Kuwait provides one of the basic indicators of the immigrant problem and also constitutes an important variable affecting the extent of the immigrant's satisfaction and stability.

The period of residence is governed by many elements. Some are connected with the immigrant himself and others are related to the laws and regulations concerned with his residence. For example, a physician having practised in Kuwait for 20 years, cannot remain for more than two extra weeks if he decides to resign his job and tries to start a private clinic. The immigrant's period of residence is also subject to the approval of his Kuwaiti sponsor who must extend his support each time the five-year permit expires. The period of residence is considered an important indicator not only regarding the stability of the immigrant manpower and production efficiency but also in the loyalty of the

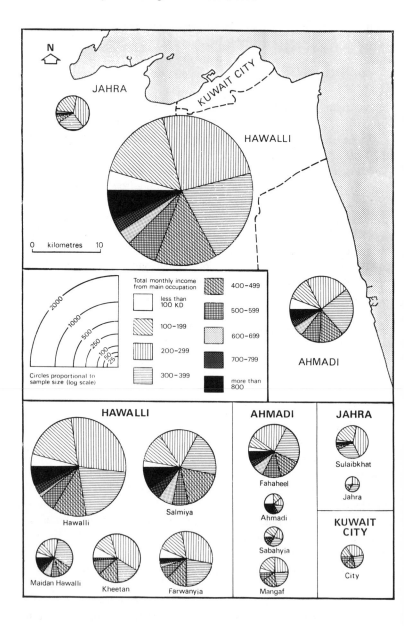

Figure 2.1   Percentage distribution of immigrant workers by period of residence and district

immigrant labourer to his job, his employer and his sponsor.

During recent years, financial considerations have had a more direct effect on residence. This was noticed particularly after the issuance of the House Lease Law allowing owners to increase property rents by up to 100 per cent every five years. This law determined the period of residence for immigrant manpower, particularly those of the lower income group who pay direct rent for housing. When the rent was increased beyond the immigrant's means, the only solution was to leave the country and this actually occurred in a number of cases.

Research showed that the Palestinians and Jordanians stay the longest, followed by other Arab groups and then the Pakistanis. Most of those staying in Kuwait for over 15 years were in those three groups (Table 1). The Palestinians have special circumstances of residence although there is no different treatment under Kuwaiti law. Their period of stay is undetermined but some leave Kuwait for other countries where a higher standard of living is possible.

The period of stay differs from one category to another just as it differs from one nationality to another. A division of manpower into unaccompanied labourers and those accompanied by families shows that the latter form around 55 per cent of the total immigrant manpower. It also shows that the unaccompanied stay for a shorter period. The 1980 Census shows that more than 45 per cent of the immigrant manpower stayed for less than five years, 23 per cent for between 5 and 9 years, 16 per cent for between 10 and 14 years and 16 per cent for 15 years or more (Table 2). A comparison of these figures from the 1980 Census with those of the Sample Survey (Table 2) shows little correlation.

Workers accompanied by their wives and children remain for longer periods. The immigration of the whole family indicates an intention to stay longer as the children will go to school. Also, the presence of the whole family in Kuwait means greater expenses and a lower rate of savings. The family will be compelled to stay for a longer period to achieve the main target of immigration, the amassing of wealth to take home, a factor which explains why 52 per cent of the sample have been in Kuwait 15 years or more (Table 2).

The period of residence in Kuwait is connected with a number of factors, the major one being job opportunities created by the State through its budget expenditures. In 1982, when State income decreased as a result of falling oil revenues, the State budget suffered a deficit of KD800 million. This resulted in job losses for both immigrant and local manpower. Following the 1982 Residence Law, 30,000 labourers left

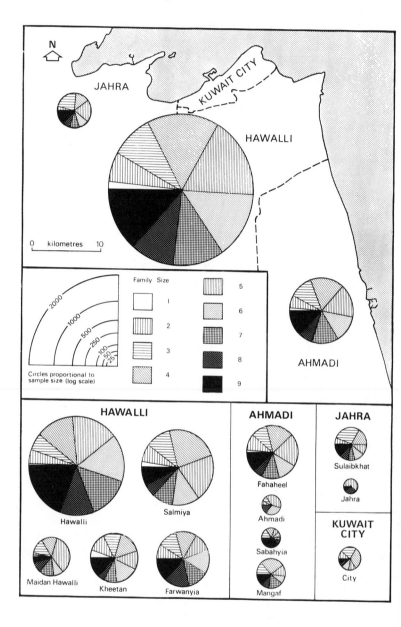

Figure 2.2   Percentage distribution of immigrant workers by marital status and district

the country having failed to obtain sponsorship (*Al Qabass Daily News* 1982). Reduction in immigration had a knock-on effect. The immigration movement influenced and reduced by economic factors resulted in a negative change in the purchasing power in some areas where these workers concentrated and led to further job losses and expulsions.

Residence in Kuwait is connected with job availability, the legal guarantee and, more importantly, is linked with the ability of the immigrant labourer to realise his determined aims. It is also related to the social status of the immigrant and the location of his home country. For example, highly qualified immigrants such as university academic staff, physicians and accountants work under contracts which entitle them to return home once a year. This category of worker tends to stay longer than the category who bear their own travel expenses. However, workers in other categories will stay if the financial rewards are high enough.

Other immigrants with short-term aims such as saving enough to build a house in their own country or to cover marriage expenses stay for short periods. These are often Iranians, neighbours to Kuwait, who have a tendency to visit their home country twice or thrice a year. In addition to the geographical advantage, Iranians are usually unaccompanied and those who establish ambitious projects which require large savings may stay for longer periods.

One group of the unskilled labour force, housemaids and servants, especially the Indians and Lebanese, have contracts which provide them with a free ticket home every other year. This group stays for short periods in Kuwait.

2.3   Educational standards

In countries like Kuwait which need a skilled immigrant labour force, the question of education is very important. Originally, immigrants came with a wide range of skills and education but unfortunately the administration was not available to plan the balance of labour nor direct it to the areas where demand was greatest. Well educated and highly skilled immigrants are in greatest demand but there is a preponderance of immigrants from the other end of the scale. 1980 records show that 24 per cent of immigrant labour is illiterate and a further 22 per cent can read and write (Table 3), though otherwise uneducated. Clearly almost half the immigrant labour force is very poorly qualified.

Frequently, immigrants take up jobs in Kuwait for which they have

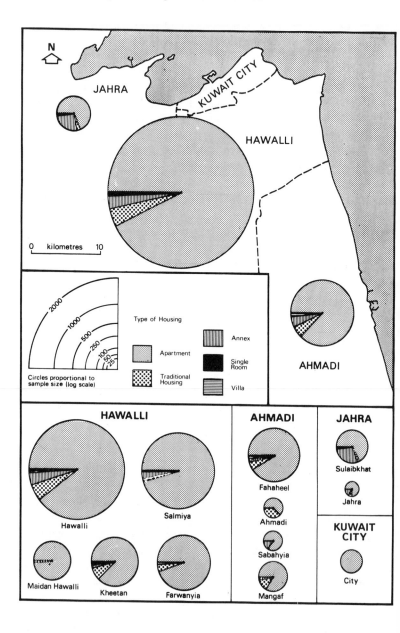

Figure 2.3 Percentage distribution of immigrant workers by educational status and district

insufficient education or training. Many of them come from poor rural areas having worked on farms, as casual labourers or been unemployed. In Kuwait they attempt, with a complete change of occupation, to fill the demand for skilled and semi-skilled workers. This retards rather than improves the development of the country.

In the sample survey only 4.5 per cent were recorded as illiterate, suggesting that the accompanied immigrant labour force is better qualified. Even so, it is interesting to see 27 per cent of the clerical posts are filled by immigrants who are illiterate or have minimal schooling (Table 4). Many of these had not been able to hold such positions in their own country (Table 5). All manual and service jobs are open to immigrants as the Kuwaitis prefer administrative jobs which carry a higher social standing. Workers of low ability are prepared to accept any post in Kuwait, being reluctant to return home to face probable unemployment.

On the other hand, immigrants of university standard held a similar proportion of scientific, technical, administrative and managerial posts in Kuwait as they did at home. Immigrants in these categories have no problems of finding employment when they return home. Table 6 illustrates this point. Some 64 per cent of illiterate and 74 per cent of barely literate groups stay for over 15 years, while only 54 per cent of those with a school education stay for a similar time. The distribution of graduates over the different time spans shows no preference. Kuwait has a greater need for skilled and professional workers with the intention to remain for many years, a stable core of such workers being essential for development. Instead, these people remain for only short periods and the illiterate and poorly qualified, for whom there is less demand and who do little to help real development of the host country, remain for many years.

2.4   Age structure

The age structure of immigrant manpower in Kuwait illustrates the ideal population pyramid of immigrants who move for work.

The 1980 Census shows 38 per cent under 30 years of age, the most active period of their life, 53 per cent between 30 and 50, and only 8 per cent over 50 years (Table 7). As the workers get older, they return home. The figures in the research sample (Table 8) for the accompanied manpower show little correlation with the Census. In this sample there were fewer under 30 (18.8 per cent) and more over 50 years of age (14.4 per cent).

The difference between the total immigrant manpower figures and those of the sample are easily explained. Bachelor labour leaves home at an early age, often with little education but plenty of physical fitness and takes up construction and labouring jobs. More elderly unaccompanied males, having reached a stage where great physical effort is not suitable, prefer to be in their own countries with their families.

In the sample group many youngsters were not seeking employment but continuing their studies while at the other end of the scale the more elderly, in white-collar occupations, could remain in their employment until they were much older (Table 9). Of greater importance is the fact that a very high proportion of the immigrant females are of childbearing age (only 3.8 per cent being over 50) thus resulting in an increase in the number of non-nationals in Kuwait.

Table 10 shows that a very high proportion of the sample were perfectly settled in Kuwait and that the small proportion who were less settled were those under 30, themselves constituting only a small proportion of the sample.

A very high proportion of the sample were unable to indicate how long they intended to stay (Table 11). Those with some plans for the future had only a short time span in view — up to five years but on the other hand others with definite ideas intended to stay for over 21 years — or for ever?

Table 9 shows the correlation of age with occupation. It must be remembered that the total immigrant workforce greatly outnumbers the local labour force so that the high proportion of immigrants in administrative positions will have a direct effect on the economic activity and organisation of policy in Kuwait. Of the sample, the under 30 group were well represented in the clerical and service occupations, the 30 to 50 age group in the scientific and technical, and the over-50s in sales and administration.

The Palestinians who made up 22 per cent of the total immigrant labour in the 1975 Census represent a majority in all age groups. Table 12 clearly illustrates their dominance in the accompanied group and highlights this increase on a percentage basis within each age group, growing from 39 per cent of the under 30s, to 42 per cent of the 30 to 40s and rising eventually to 54 per cent of the over-50 category. No other nationality shows an increase in this way.

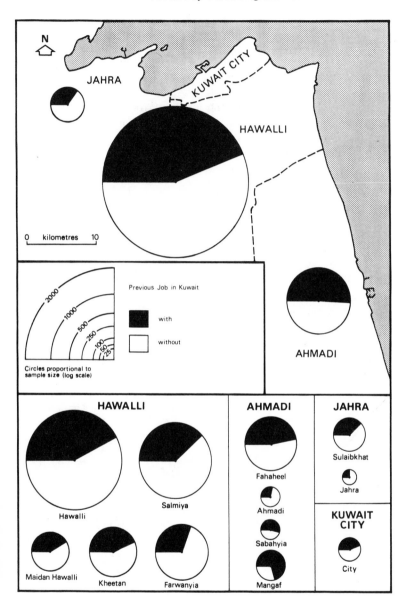

Figure 2.4   Percentage distribution of immigrant workforce by sex and district

2.5   Sex structure

The sex structure of manpower is considered an important indicator of the socio-economic trends of society. Participation of women in the labour force is a characteristic of the immigrant community. Women make up only 3 per cent of the local workforce but 12 per cent of gainfully employed immigrant manpower. Although Kuwaiti women are not prevented from working, their contribution is in fact very low due to poor educational standards. This creates more favourable circumstances for the immigrant women.

The survey showed that sex structure is closely related to age structure. Females are concentrated in the younger categories and males in the older categories. Around 15 per cent of males and 39 per cent of females belong to the under-30 age group, 35 per cent of males and 16 per cent of females belong to the 40-49 age group but in the over-50 category males predominate. The single persons mainly below marriageable age are part of the families accompanying the 88 per cent of males (Tables 8 and 13). Sex structure shows less relation to educational standards. The females have a higher educational standard, around 35 per cent having received a good schooling, while males with the same qualifications form only 24 per cent. Females with a university degree are 38 per cent against 33 per cent of males (Table 14). This may be explained by the fact that females are normally employed in educational, scientific or technical jobs which require minimum entrance qualifications rather than in manual roles. Immigrant working women play an important role in supporting the economic activity of the country. Table 15 shows their percentage participation in the various occupational sectors. However, their importance must not be overstressed as women constitute only 17.2 per cent of the sample (Table 8) and only 13 per cent of the *total* foreign labour force in 1980 (Table 7).

Females tend to stay for a shorter period due to social ties. The study shows the average stay period for females is almost 10 years while that for males is 13 years. Averages, however, hide the fact that around 57 per cent of males stay for more than 15 years in the country while only 30 per cent of the females stay that long; also, 12 per cent of the males but 28 per cent of the females stay for under 5 years (Table 16).

Few respondents were capable of determining the period of their stay in Kuwait, comprising only 25 per cent of the females and 16 per cent of the males. Of these, the women intended to stay for a shorter time (Table 17).

2.6   Occupational structure of the immigrant workforce

During the 1950s it was the Kuwaiti Government's intention to use its oil revenues to provide basic services and the necessary infrastructure which the country lacked at that time. This involved the establishment of different government bodies to supervise the establishment of these projects. The available local labour force was not able to cope and the result was an inflow of foreign manpower in large numbers to join the building and construction sector, and to meet growing demand for services. The urgency of the work and the pressure on the administration resulted in poorly planned projects and extensive expenditure. Demand was so great that immigrants were placed in positions for which they had neither qualifications nor experience.

Amid the rush to employ immigrant labour force in the sectors mentioned above, other important areas of the economy such as commerce, manufacturing, agriculture, transportation and communication were neglected. This resulted in imbalances, with a large number of both foreign and local labourers being employed in building, construction and service sectors while other sectors remained with an inadequate labour force.

To illustrate the imbalance, comparison was made of the number of immigrant workers in selected sectors during 1957 and 1980 to show the change in the numerical distribution of the labour force. For example, between 1957 and 1980 the number engaged in agriculture and fishing increased from 446 to 5,212 (an increase of 1,070 per cent). Mining and quarrying showed the least increase; the number of employees engaged in this sector increased from only 4,194 to 4,262 (an increase of 1.6 per cent), this being due to the poorness of these natural resources in Kuwait. The wholesale and retail trades showed the highest increase (1,222 per cent), depicting a change from 4,073 in 1957 to 53,840 in 1980. Building and construction showed the second highest increase (1,094 per cent), from 8,025 to 95,893. Transportation and communications showed a change of 987 per cent and manufacturing industry an increase of 582 per cent. The service sector, which employed the largest immigrant and local workforce, increased by 396 per cent (Table 18). One characteristic of the above statistics is the predominance of males. The females amount to only 3 per cent of the total labour force, the majority being engaged in the service sector.

During the same period, 1957-1980, significant changes took place in the relative share of the immigrant labour force in certain occupations. These in turn reflected the structural changes which occurred in

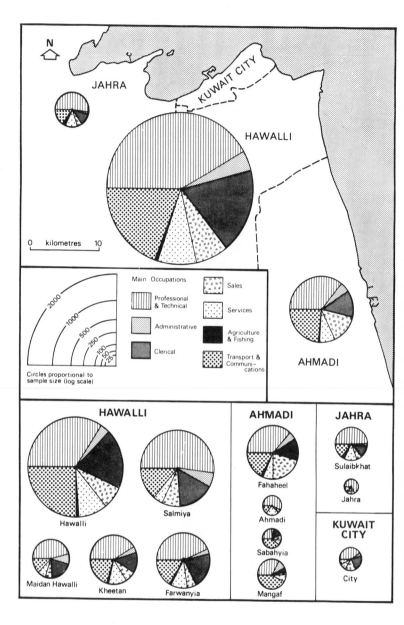

Figure 2.5   Percentage distribution of main occupations of immigrant workers by district

the economic activities. Outlined here are changes in three major occupations, namely, the professional and technical workers, service workers and lastly production workers and labourers. Whereas in 1957 production labourers were 67.2 per cent of the immigrant labour force, in 1980 they were only 44.6 per cent, despite a numerical rise of over 131,000. Professional and technical workers were 16.4 per cent instead of 5.8 per cent. Service workers rose from 9 per cent to 20.3 per cent of immigrant workers (Table 19). Clearly, despite attempts at 'Kuwaitization', Kuwaitis are still heavily clustered in two areas of activity, namely 'executive' and 'services', accounting in 1980 for 59.9 per cent of the total employed indigenous labour force (Table 20). The comparable figures for the non-Kuwaitis being 36.7 per cent (Table 19). Within an overall situation of a declining contribution to the labour force; 33.1 per cent in 1957, 29.1 per cent in 1975 and 21.4 per cent in 1980 Kuwaitis were out-numbered in all employment categories with the sole exception of agriculture and fisheries and trade in 1957, and of agriculture and fisheries in 1975. In effect, even in those areas of economic activity where Kuwaitis have been most disposed towards employment, they have become a minority.

The reverse side of the coin was demonstrated by the role of the foreign workforce. There was increasingly no function performed within the country where the expatriate community could be dispensed with without serious upheaval. In the senior echelons of the employment structure the input of the foreign component of the labour force was critical, providing in 1975 71 per cent and in 1980 79 per cent of all personnel in the professional and technical grades (Annual Statistical Abstract 1982).

Similar considerations applied to the numerically smaller administrative and clerical grades. At the manual end of the employment spectrum, the non-Kuwaitis' role was no less significant, with more than 85 per cent of labourers and manual production workers supplied from outside in 1975. The comparable figure for 1980 was 92 per cent, indicating a deterioration in Kuwaiti self-sufficiency in this area (*Annual Statistical Abstract*, 1982).

Interesting contrasts can also be made on the variations between the spread of activities of the expatriate labour force as a whole and that of the foreign employees resident in Kuwait accompanied by their families. The consistent pattern over the last decade has been for the main area of concern to be the labourer and production worker category (Table 20), with further concentrations in the services and professional and scientific grades. Distributions among the workers resident in Kuwait with their families is different from the norm for the foreign workforce as a whole. Here, the clustering is towards the professional and technical level (64.3 per cent) with only a small secondary peaking in the labourer and production worker grade (22 per cent).

There is an element of predictability in this skewed pattern. Legal constraints tend to favour better paid workers in bringing their families with them to Kuwait. Equally important, those in the upper echelons of the employment hierarchy can better afford to cover the costs attendant on their maintaining their families in Kuwait, while lesser paid workers have both the need to economise on expenditures in Kuwait and the requirement to maximise their savings while in Kuwait since their disposable income is far less than that of the upper cadres of the foreign labour force. It is also a truism that, the longer expatriates remain in Kuwait, and the workforce accompanied by family tends to have a longer mean stay than that without family (Table 2), the better the level of employment attained through seniority, promotion and improved information on available opportunities. The situation is reinforced by considerations of age pyramids for the two groups. The accompanied foreign workers tend to be clustered in the older age cohorts while the unaccompanied expatriates are, on average, slightly younger and the less likely to be married. But, while structural differences between the groups are important in explaining the strong bias away from the norm by the accompanied workers, the economic aspects cannot be ignored. Kuwait has become an expensive place for foreigners to live *vis-à-vis* alternatives elsewhere. Few foreign workers other than those in well paid employment could consider the costs of residence, including accommodation, health, educational and overhead costs, for their families as feasible. It is a not inconsiderable factor, too, that major public works have been provided with labour through direct supply contracts with South and South East Asian companies, within which there is only limited opportunity for accompanied residence in Kuwait.

For a variety of reasons, therefore, Kuwait has moved to a position where its foreign labour force is increasingly made up of single, mainly bachelor, personnel. At the 1980 Census, 30.8 per cent of the immigrants were unaccompanied, in contrast with 28.3 per cent five years earlier. There is a persistent immaturity affecting the expatriate working community as a result which, while it has the advantage of limiting the propensity of expatriates to remain in Kuwait, has the disadvantage of inhibiting the growth of a balanced indigenous workforce across the gamut of occupations, especially in respect of the lower paid manual jobs.

2.7   Occupations of immigrant workforce in their home country

The sample study investigated 1,043 immigrants who had worked in their home country. Out of these, 44.4 per cent had been engaged in professional and technical professions, 4.2 per cent as administrative and managerial workers, 12.1 per cent as clerks, 7.4 per cent as sales workers, 4.3 per cent as service workers, 9.8 per cent as fishing and agricultural workers, while 17.8 per cent had been engaged in production work and transportation (Table 21).

The distribution by nationality shows that 53 per cent of the Palestinians and Jordanians were in employment before coming to Kuwait. Of those employed, 32.7 per cent were working as professional and technical workers, only 1.2 per cent as administrative and management workers, and 19.9 per cent as agricultural and fishery workers, a high figure due to the majority of workers in this nationality coming from rural areas. In addition, 9.2 per cent were working as clerks and 22.3 per cent as transportation and production workers.

Statistics for the Egyptians reveal a large proportion of the immigrants (80.7 per cent) who had had employment in their home country. This is much greater than that recorded for Palestinians, who are regarded as a special case among immigrants to Kuwait. Among the Egyptians 66.6 per cent have worked in their country as professional and technical workers, 14.1 per cent as clerks (which goes in accordance with their economic activities in Kuwait) and 6.4 per cent as administrative and managerial workers.

Among non-Arabs, 80 per cent of Indians had been employed before. The immigrant Indians have been engaged in three occupations in their home country: 38.7 per cent have been professional and technical workers, 27 per cent clerks, and 21 per cent production and transportation workers.

As for Pakistanis, we find that 61.7 per cent had had employment in their own country. 52.4 per cent worked as production and transportation workers, 33.3 per cent as professional workers and 9.5 per cent in sales. The Pakistanis are not found in administration and managerial work, services, and agriculture and fishery. The Pakistani and Indian immigrants are reluctant to join service work due to language and social barriers. These two nationalities are concentrated in professional and technical work, as labourers, and in transportation due to their experience in the field and knowledge of the English language. Europeans are concentrated in professional and scientific work (84 per cent) and administration (8 per cent) and do not feature in the other

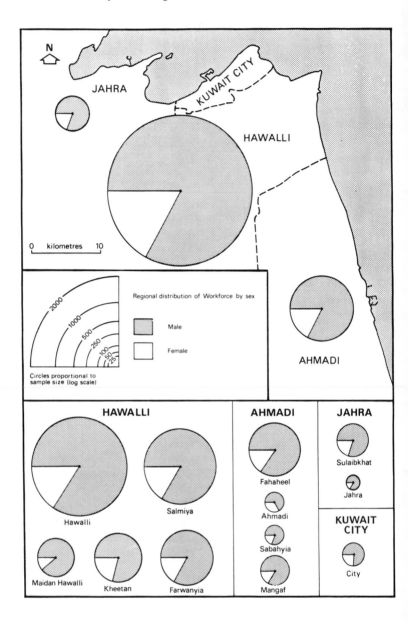

Figure 2.6　Percentage distribution of immigrant workers by employment status and district

categories. The majority of the European immigrants have practised various professions in their home countries (92.6 per cent) (Table 21).

2.8   Occupations of the immigrant workforce in Kuwait

Our study revealed that there is some similarity between the jobs which were practised by immigrants in their home countries and the ones being practised in Kuwait, mainly in three occupations, namely, professional and technical work, clerical work, and production and transportation work. In this respect, the proportion of the sample employed in professional and technical works increased from 44.4 per cent to 46.5 per cent, and in clerical increased from 12.1 per cent to 12.9 per cent. Production and transportation work increased from 17.8 to 21.8 per cent. One category where more significant variations appeared was agriculture and fisheries with a decrease from 9.8 per cent to 0.9 per cent (Tables 21 and 22).

Despite attempts to promote agricultural expansion in areas such as Shegaici, Abdualli and Wafra, of the 102 workers who farmed in their own country only 10 practised farming in Kuwait, other occupations being more attractive. On the other hand, the numbers of those participating in service jobs almost doubled from 46 workers in the profession in their own country to 145 workers in Kuwait.

There has been in general a redistribution of the occupations practised by immigrants. In Kuwait opportunities exist for improvement in status, many immigrants, as we have shown earlier, holding jobs for which they are not adequately qualified.

The study shows that the Palestinian and Jordanian labour force are engaged mainly in three occupations, namely, technical, production and transportation, and clerical jobs. The proportion of their labour force in these three areas accounts for 80.0 per cent of the total Palestinian and Jordanian manpower in Kuwait. Of this, 35.8 per cent are in technical jobs, 25.0 per cent in production and transportation, and 19.0 per cent in clerical jobs. It is worth mentioning that their share in clerical jobs shows a significant shift from 9.2 per cent in their country of origin to 19.0 per cent in Kuwait. In agriculture and fishing, however, they show a drop from 20.0 per cent to 1.3 per cent, which is due to the lesser importance of this sector in Kuwait.

The Egyptian labour force in our study has two main occupations, professional and technical, and clerical, accounting for 83.1 per cent of the total Egyptian labour force in the country. Egyptians are predominant in the public sector, in medical, teaching, engineering, secretarial and clerical jobs, and are rarely found in agriculture and fishing. Moreover, unlike the Syrians and Lebanese, Egyptians are rarely found in executive, management and sales jobs. The change observed among the Egyptian labour force is in administrative and managerial jobs where their proportions in Kuwait drop to 2.0 per cent from the 6.4 per cent recorded in their country of origin.

Arabs, other than Egyptians, a group mainly comprised of Iraqis, Syrians and Lebanese, are quite evenly distributed among most occupations except agriculture and fisheries. They predominate in sales and service jobs in general, and are noticeably smaller in number in scientific and technical occupations. The change in the occupational structure of this group is observed in three sectors. First, there is a decrease from 34 per cent of immigrants holding technical and professional jobs in their home country to 24 per cent holding the same jobs in Kuwait. In services, the proportion increased from 3.6 per cent at home to 12 per cent in Kuwait. While 8.4 per cent of this group were in agriculture at home, few continued with the same occupation in Kuwait.

Indians predominate in medical, laboratory, nursing, electronic and secretarial jobs. They are found mostly in jobs where the English language is used, especially in companies and corporations which deal with foreign sources. There is no significant change in their occupational structure regarding Kuwait and their country of origin.

The Pakistani labour force is predominant in production and transportation, and technical and scientific jobs. Their contribution in services and agriculture is nil. A significant change is observed in the occupational structure of the Pakistani labour force in their country and in Kuwait. Although their role in administrative and managerial jobs is negligible in their own country, they score 6.0 per cent in Kuwait. Moreover, their share in clerical jobs in their own country is 4.8 per cent, while in Kuwait it is 15.2 per cent. Their share in transportation and production drops from 52.4 per cent to 45.5 per cent.

Asians, other than those mentioned, are found in two occupations, services, where their share is 33.3 per cent, and production and transportation, where their share reaches 35.1 per cent. This differed from what they did in their home country, where they had no role in the service sector and a much higher proportion in production and transportation (45.6 per cent). In contrast, 13.6 per cent were in agriculture and fishing at home while their role in this sector in Kuwait is nil (Table 22).

No variation is observed in the occupational structure of the

European labour force which works mainly in the scientific and technical sectors.

The considerable variations between the roles played by immigrants in their countries of origin and in Kuwait gives cause for concern. In almost every case of variation the new role taken by the worker requires a higher standard of qualification and training. This suggests that immigrants are taking jobs for which they do not have adequate qualifications, a serious factor in impeding the development of Kuwait.

References

Al Qabass Daily News, No. 1763, Nov. 3, 1982.
Annual Statistical Abstract, 1982.

3 SOCIAL FACTORS RELEVANT TO IMMIGRANT WORKERS

3.1 Geographical distribution of immigrants by nationality

The geographical distribution of the population in Kuwait is governed by the administrative and social aspects of the country. In this sense, the placement of the population in different areas of the country is not linked to the productivity of these areas or any other locational factor. It is largely affected by the nature of the country's economy, which is service oriented.

The importance of studying both the Kuwaiti and non-Kuwaiti population distributions stems from the fact that the majority of the country's population are immigrants. However, the distribution of the population is not ruled by the economic activities of the actively employed manpower and hence the pattern of travel to and from work is not the same as most other countries.

Kuwait City provides 80.0 per cent of the total jobs in the country with 12.4 per cent of the country's population, out of which 60.7 per cent are immigrants. From a total of 3,321 economic establishments in 1980, Kuwait City provided 1,762, which represents 44.0 per cent of the total, with 103,843 employees representing 50.5 per cent of the total labour force working in the country's economic establishments.

Table 23 depicts the existing relation between areas of population concentration and the sites of economic activity. The Capital Governorate contains 12.7 per cent of the total Kuwaiti population and 34.4 per cent of the total Kuwaiti labour force. It also contains 13.9 per cent of all immigrants and 51.1 per cent of the immigrant labour force.

Most Kuwaitis live in Hawalli Governorate (36.4 per cent) and most immigrants too (68.7 per cent). These people represent a small proportion of the Kuwaiti labour force (9.1 per cent) and a much larger proportion of the immigrant labour force (26.9 per cent). Ahmadi Governorate houses 24.1 per cent of all Kuwaitis and 12.2 per cent of all immigrants, these being a very large proportion of the Kuwaiti labour force (50.9 per cent) and of the immigrant workers (16.2 per cent). The final Governorate, Jahra, houses about a quarter of all Kuwaitis and only a small proportion of immigrants (5.2 per cent).

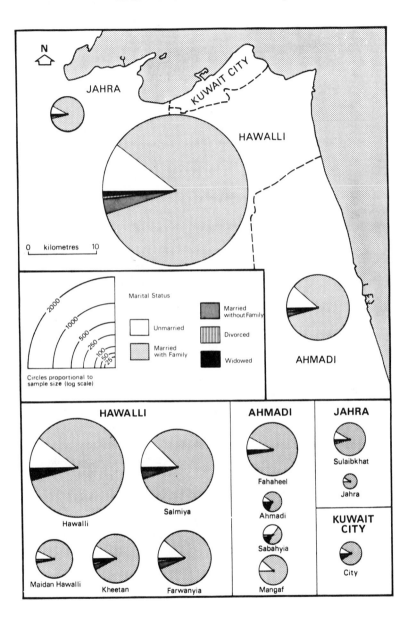

Figure 3.1 Percentage distribution of immigrant workers by nationality and district

The residents in Jahra Governorate provide very few workers, 5.5 per cent and 5.8 per cent, respectively.

Table 23   The geographical distribution of the total population and labour force in economic establishments in the four Governorates (1980)

| | Population | | Employees | |
	Kuwaitis	Immigrants	Kuwaitis	Immigrants
Capital	12.7	13.9	34.4	51.1
Hawalli	36.4	68.7	9.1	26.9
Ahmadi	24.1	12.2	50.9	16.2
Jahra	26.7	5.2	5.5	5.8
Total	100.0	100.0	100.0	100.0

Source: 1980 Census.

The immigrant labour force is concentrated mainly in three sectors, namely, manufacturing industry, construction and building and services. These three sectors comprise 75.8 per cent of the total immigrant labour force. These sectors, however, are not situated according to the geographical distribution of the country's population. The construction and building sector, which employs the majority of the immigrant labour force, is distributed in many different localities, for example, construction of Kuwait housing areas, construction of roads and bridges and commercial complexes. It is known that the immigrant labour force involved in this industry is accommodated in old dwellings, abandoned by Kuwaitis around Kuwait City, Hawalli and Kheetan, and beside the Korean immigrant camps in South Fahaheel.

The manufacturing industry sector is concentrated in Shuwaikh and the Ray area, which is a geographical extension of Shuwaikh. The other location is in Shuaiba in the eastern coastal area. In fact, most of these manufacturing areas are not surrounded by residential areas, the labourers coming from a wide area.

The service sector is centred in the town of Kuwait, where the government departments and private firms are located. The population of the capital is less by far than its workforce.

The geographical distribution of the workforce may not be accounted for according to nationality. Rents and the availability of accommodation are the correct criteria.

The 1980 Census made it impossible to recognize the most recent residential areas of the immigrant labour force as it omitted the geographical distribution on a basis of nationality included in previous censuses. In the following discussion we will depend on the 1975 Census and the results of our field study to emphasise the concentrations in certain areas.

Geographical distribution in the 1975 Census

The main areas inhabited by immigrants are Hawalli, Salmiya, Farwaniya and Kuwait Town. Hawalli is given as the residence for 23 per cent of all immigrants, Salmiya houses 18.6 per cent, Kuwait Town 12.7 per cent and both Kheetan and Farwaniya 6.7 per cent. In particular areas the immigrants make up a very high proportion of the population. Immigrants form 92 per cent of the total population of both Hawalli and Maidan Hawalli, 85 per cent of the total population of Kuwait Town and 78 per cent of Farwaniya (Annual Statistical Abstract 1981).

Table 24 shows the details of immigrant residence by nationality. 78.6 per cent of Palestinians and Jordanians are concentrated in four areas of Kuwait, 35.5 per cent live in Hawalli, where they make up 60.0 per cent of the immigrant population there, 20.8 per cent live in Salmiya, where they make up 44.0 per cent, and 12.8 live in Farwaniya, where they make up 74 per cent of the total immigrant population of the town. Kheetan, the fourth area, houses 9.5 per cent of them and they make up 55.0 per cent of Kheetan's immigrant residents.

71.8 per cent of the Egyptians are concentrated in four areas too, namely Kuwait Town, Salmiya, Hawalli and Maidan Hawalli with 21.5, 25.4, 18.9 and 6.0 per cent respectively of their total numbers. The explanation for the concentration of the Egyptians in Kuwait Town is that they took up residence there in older Kuwaiti dwellings which are not yet re-developed. The immigrant Egyptians, usually bachelors, share rooms in these dwellings with up to 500 persons per house.

The rest of the Arabs, represented by and large by Iraqis, Lebanese and Syrians, are concentrated in Hawalli, Kuwait Town and Kheetan, most being found in Hawalli (22.2 per cent), where they make up 20.4 per cent of all immigrants and 19 per cent of the total population.

The Iranians, among the earliest immigrants and having strong mutual social and economic ties, are known to be among the majority of non-Arab immigrants in Kuwait, according to the 1975 Census. 26.3 per cent of them live in Kuwait Town. In some sections of the town they make up a high proportion of the immigrant population, 35 per cent in Salwa, 31.0 per cent in Ray and 30 per cent in Jabriya.

The geographical distribution of Indians resembles that of the Iranians. Their concentration in Kuwait Town, Salmiya and Hawalli is respectively 39.3, 13.7 and 6.4 per cent of their total numbers. In

Kuwait Town where they make up 16.1 per cent of the total population, they are employed as housemaids and servants.

The Pakistanis are found in similar areas to the Iranians and Indians with an additional location, Farwaniya. Some 60.0 per cent of them are found in Kuwait Town, Salmiya, Farwaniya and Hawalli. They show no definite concentrations except in Jaleeb Al Shuyukh, where they make up to 19.0 per cent of the total population. An examination of Table 24 will provide further information on immigrant distribution in 1975.

Geographical distribution in Sample Survey 1981

In many ways the geographical distribution of the immigrant labour force shows a positive correlation with the distribution of the population in general.

The Palestinians and Jordanians comprise the majority in all areas where immigrants are found. Their main concentrations are in Hawalli and Farwaniya where they make up about 53 per cent of all immigrants in both of those areas, in Mangaf where they comprise 68 per cent and in Salmiya and Kheetan where they comprise 38 and 37 per cent (Table 25). Of the 761 Palestinians and Jordanians in our survey 41 per cent live in Hawalli, 18 per cent in Salmiya and 13 per cent in Farwaniya.

Most of the immigrant Egyptians in our survey live in Hawalli (28 per cent) and Salmiya (27 per cent) although they make higher percentages of immigrants in Sulaibikhat (39 per cent), Farwaniya (31 per cent) and Salmiya (30 per cent). Most of the other Arabs in the survey live in Hawalli (40 per cent) but make up 31 per cent of immigrants in Maidan Hawalli. Of the non-Arabs, most Indians (40 per cent) live in Kuwait City, making 72 per cent of the immigrant population there. 55 per cent of our sample immigrants live in either Hawalli or Salmiya with 10 per cent in Fahaheel.

It is clear that the immigrants are concentrated mainly in Hawalli, Salmiya, Kheetan and Farwaniya. These areas are considered to be immigrant areas where the Kuwaiti landowners have invested their money in erecting particular buildings for them. These differ greatly from the Kuwaiti residential areas which are really suburbs of the town, pure residential areas, unlike the immigrant areas where both residential and commercial services are found.

3.2   Education and the labour force

The government provides free educational services for the large expatriate community as well as for Kuwaitis. However, in recent years the government has been forced to limit expansion in free public education.

This decision was made in the light of the rapid growth in student numbers, in addition to a manpower shortage among teachers. In this respect the 1982 statistics (Annual Statistical Abstract 1982) Table 26 show that, from a total of 23,158 teachers working in public schools, kindergarten to secondary level, the Kuwaiti share was 28 per cent against Egyptian 43 per cent and Palestinian 22.5 per cent. In technical education, the Kuwaiti teachers represented 10.8 per cent from a total of 1,209 teachers. The increasing cost of public education is shown by the high expenditure of the Ministry of Education, which amounted in 1981/82 to KD221,500 million, 7.4 per cent of the total general budget expenditure, while in the fiscal year 1977/78 government expenditure on public education amounted to only KD116,038 million.

Table 26   Origin of teachers by nationality 1981/82

Nationality	Male Number	Female Number	Total Number	%
Kuwaiti	2,146	4,332	6,478	28.0
Egyptian	4,805	5,168	9,973	43.1
Jordanian and Palestinian	3,104	2,114	5,218	22.5
Iraqi	104	136	240	1.0
Lebanese	41	47	88	0.4
Syrian	603	243	846	3.6
Others	145	170	315	1.4
Total	10,948	12,210	23,158	100.0

Source: *Annual Statistical Abstract*, 1982, Ministry of Planning, p. 312.

In 1981/82 the number of students among the immigrant community reached 160,924 constituting 49.9 per cent of a total of 322,512 students in both general and technical schools. Because of these large numbers, 50 per cent of the total expenditure allocated for public education goes to meet the various educational needs of the immigrant community. The educational services were affected by the economic problems resulting from reduced oil revenues. In 1983 the government stopped distributing school uniforms and the daily free meals.

University education is free for all students. The number of Kuwaiti

University students in 1981/82 was 10,340, with 33.3 per cent being immigrant students, while in the same year in Kuwait University only 25 per cent of the total teachers and instructors, 677 in all, were Kuwaiti. The University budget, which is independent from that allocated to the Ministry of Education, amounted to KD55 million for the fiscal year 1981/82.

The new immigrants who came after the government decision to limit the enrolment of immigrant students in public schools faced difficulties in finding schools for their children. This problem was solved in two ways. The first was by running evening classes in each school. This also put additional financial burdens on the government as these evening classes use the same manpower and equipment facilities as the daytime schools. The second way was by opening private schools to serve the large immigrant community. These schools represent a wide range of nationalities. Although the Ministry of Education super-vises private education, each nationality uses its own language, systems and methods of education. The emergence of the private education system has led to some internal problems, especially when Kuwaiti students were prevented from enrolling in the non-Arab private schools.

The private education system has also recorded rapid growth in recent years. Numbers in private schools increased from 9,856 students in 1966/67 to 69,296 in 1981/82, a 600 per cent increase during the period. The number of teachers in these schools increased from 387 in 1966/67 to 3,448 teachers in 1981/82, an increase of 790 per cent.

The number of private schools in the four school levels reached 202 schools in 1981/82. Out of this, 108 were Arabic and 94 foreign schools with instruction in a language other than Arabic. The recorded number of public government schools in the same year was 471. The large number of private schools for varying nationalities has, no doubt, certain socio-economic and political effects, though not all of them adverse.

The various implications of the educational sector

One of the characteristics of the education sector in Kuwait is the general tendency of the immigrant students to join scientific and technical studies while Kuwaitis join art and theoretical studies. A clear evaluation cannot be made, however, due to the government decision not to enrol in technical school a proportion of immigrants exceeding 20 per cent of the Kuwaitis applying for registration in technical schools and institutes.[1] This is illustrated by the 1981/82 statistics which show that the total enrolment in technical education was 5,750, of which 929 were immigrants. In spite of these restrictions, Kuwait is highly regarded among the Gulf States for encouraging expatriate students to enrol in technical studies. In this respect the Kuwait Government pay incentives for immigrant students joining technical schools and technical institutions.[2]

The students' study preferences can be analysed from enrolments in colleges of Kuwait University. In this respect, immigrant students have a greater tendency to join scientific colleges. The 1981/82 statistics reveal that the number of immigrant students in the Faculty of Science was 42 per cent of the total enrolment in the Faculty, and 50 and 36 per cent in Engineering and Medicine, respectively. On the other hand, immigrant student enrolment in Faculties of Art, Law and Commerce and Economics and Politics was lower at 13, 20 and 17 per cent of the enrolment in these faculties respectively.

This tendency among the immigrant students meets the need of the country for specialized manpower especially in scientific and technical fields. On the other hand, the Kuwaitis who will form the future local manpower are still affected by traditional socio-economic and political values which despise technical professions and hence are reluctant to join technical education. So, professional preferences among Kuwaitis have affected their educational attitude. This is reflected in the distribution of the country's labour force, where, for example, white-collar government jobs occupy 45 per cent of the Kuwaiti labour force but only 23 per cent of the immigrant labour force.

The social relations, wage levels and the size of immigrations are the major aspects which affect the attitude of the Kuwaiti labour force. Immigrant students representing various nationalities are found in all levels of studies within schools. Palestinians and Jordanians constitute 50 per cent of the total students in public schools, while Egyptians, Iraqis, Syrians and Lebanese constitute 5.7, 3.8, 8.0 and 3.0 per cent, respectively. Kuwaiti students are poorly represented in schools in predominantly immigrant areas and are often in the minority even in 'Kuwaiti' areas.

Palestinians usually score outstanding results in all study stages. In the 1981/82 examinations the best fifty students were immigrants, underlining the fact that immigrant students who succeed in gaining university places are of a very high standard. Such results have led to the erroneous belief that Kuwaiti students are spoiled by the high living standards and economic security which in turn leads to negative effects.

The Kuwaiti student finds real difficulty with the different Arabic used in teaching, especially during primary education, but slowly becomes familiar with the language as he proceeds in his education and becomes more mature.

The main problem of education stems from the scarcity of Kuwaiti teachers and a large majority of immigrant students. This is a vicious circle worth further discussion.

Kuwaitis are reluctant to join the educational field as the school-teacher is losing his social privileges and status and lacks independence in decision-making within the school. He is answerable to a series of supervisors from the headmaster to the Ministry's Under Secretary. Added to this is the economic hardship of the profession. The government solution to this problem was to grant incentives for Kuwaiti teachers as a compensation (25 per cent of the basic salary). However, this one-sided action was taken by the non-Kuwaiti teachers as discrimination and an injustice and did not result in any improvement in the situation. The establishment of a Teaching Institute which accepted intermediate school students was unfortunately unable to provide good standard teachers so this institution no longer exists.

The Teachers Training Institute accepts secondary school graduates for a two-year training during which the student is paid KD100. Despite this support and training their teaching standard is very low especially in comparison to immigrant teachers who are usually university graduates with much more skill and experience. This has created a division between Kuwaiti and non-Kuwaiti teachers which is in turn reflected in the educational system in the country.

The discussion of the problems of Kuwaiti manpower in educational fields is important because of its impact on the immigrant teachers and students. Continuous change in the Kuwaiti education system has led to the lowering of the performance level of many immigrant teachers to below that recorded in their home countries. The unsettled educational system and exposure to trial and error in the curriculum may jeopardise the educational standard of all students.

3.3   Social problems arising from the presence of the immigrant workforce in Kuwait

The problems which arise here are impossible to quantify. Nevertheless, this is a very important part of the study which covers the social aspects of the labour force and tries to pin-point the social problem created by a majority of non-Kuwaitis in the population.

There is no country in the world today where the labour force is completely formed of nationals. Advancements in communications and transport have made the movement of large numbers of people across national borders very easy and they often move despite restrictions imposed by the host country, especially if the movements are job orientated.

Immigration to Kuwait is solely induced by the existing job opportunities and results in the very important fact that the immigrant labour force now constitutes 77 per cent of the country's total labour force and 58 per cent of the country's population. This point must not be overlooked when discussing economic or political issues in Kuwait.

The immigrant labour force is a majority in all sectors of the economy, both private and government. In such a situation, Kuwaitis feel compelled to compete with foreigners in all jobs within all sectors. This is so even though there is a commitment from the government to fill up gradually with Kuwaitis the posts at present occupied by immigrant workers. The government policy of Kuwaitization has probably created as many problems as it was intended to cure. Firstly, it lowered productivity across the complete spectrum of the labour force; in the Kuwaitis who knew they would eventually gain promotion whatever their productivity and in the non-Kuwaitis who knew their chances of promotion were slim however hard they worked. Kuwaiti nationals, it will be recalled, are secure in the knowledge that they are guaranteed employment.

Secondly, posts in the higher grades of administration require more educational qualifications and experience than the Kuwaitis possess. Government policy was, therefore, geared towards placing into posts of importance staff unable to do the job adequately, this being aggravated in the civil service by regulations indicating promotion on time priority rather than qualification. As a consequence, the promotion of Kuwaitis did not follow a normal ranking and career path. All this led to negative effects on the professional structure and labour performance (Al-Motawa 1983) and in addition resulted in much social prejudice.

The concept of 'a job' was itself a new phenomenon in Kuwait and was only introduced after the discovery of oil and the need to fill government posts to administer this new wealth. This, from its inception, changed the social relationships in the Kuwaiti communities themselves, especially so in the absence of distinct job ranking and clear promotion systems. The inflow of immigrants deepened these social problems still further. Low productivity among the Kuwaiti labour force has been explained by some researchers with the hypothesis that the Kuwaitis often think that the payment received is a rightful share of the national wealth and has nothing to do with job performance or productivity (Al-Motawa 1983). More likely is the explanation that promotion is not related to performance so there is no incentive to work harder or even gain further qualifications or skills.

Additionally, the Kuwaitis work with a majority of other nationals. It is understood that the Kuwaitis will receive early promotion and the other members of the workforce, in an attempt to gain good connections with the eventual supervisors, will even absorb their work load so making the Kuwaitis even less productive and content to neglect their duties.

The growth rate forecast for domestic product is far beyond the scope of the Kuwaitis even combined with the present large immigrant labour force and a greater proportion of immigrant workers will be required, leading no doubt to further imbalances and social problems. The Kuwaitis who are expected by society to improve productivity and performance, to take leading roles in all spheres and to control the country's administration find themselves in an impossible situation.

The recorded growth in labour productivity was one per cent between 1965-80 and was constant around this average but sometimes dropped to 0.5 per cent in individual years. Some forecasts show that the growth in the Kuwait labour force will be below 3.9 per cent until the year 2000. This should certainly be considered when forecasting future demands on total labour force to avoid any serious gap in the provision of the Kuwaiti and the immigrant workforce. Productivity is not improved by increasing the number of workers but by increasing the skills of the workers and using their qualities to the best advantage for the country. Examination is certainly required of the real needs of the country and an exposure of the existing disguised unemployment which prevails. Additional workers are required but, as outlined below, are often filling positions that need never have been created.

The immigration of workers who are sometimes unnecessary creates a situation which is worsened day after day, creating a vicious circle getting beyond the control of the government. It builds upon itself, as in the case of agencies run by immigrants to organise the immigration of domestic labour.

The inflow of Asians from the Philippines and Korea added a new category of immigrant with different languages, cultures and social habits. Their immigration was induced by the higher expenditure level appearing after the oil boom of 1973. It was also linked to the implementation of projects such as highways and flyovers built to solve the country's traffic problems. Traffic problems which, in any case, should have been solved by a geographical relocation of services and government establishments instead of concentrating them around Kuwait City.

The inflow of the Asian labourers mentioned above was accompanied (as if in coincidence) by Asian female immigrants who came to work as housemaids. There is no logical explanation for the sudden shift towards these new nationalities, especially as they earn double the salaries earned by the Indians and Pakistanis and brought new problems of communication, new cultures and social habits.

A symposium on 'The role of the foreign labour force in the Arab Gulf States', organised by the Arab Institute for Planning in Kuwait and the Centre of the Arab Union Studies, January 1983, highlighted the social unrest brought about by the high number of immigrants and by the newer categories of immigrants. There is concern that, whereas the traditional immigrants with historical, geographical and social ties with Kuwait (Al-Moosa 1983) have become an accepted part of Kuwaiti life, these newer immigrants with different characteristics may result in further socio-economic or even political disturbance. It is feared that the whole issue of immigrant labour is being mishandled and that this will seriously affect the country's future economy and development.

Educational aspects and the socio-economic factors which encouraged Kuwaitis to avoid technical and scientific studies were outlined in our earlier discussion. The professional pyramid which formed as a result of this was different from that found in other industrial countries, theirs reflecting economic need while that of Kuwait reflected reluctance to participate. Immigrants were always available and willing to fill any posts in this or any other sector found disagreeable to the Kuwaitis themselves.

While there are immigrants to do the work, the Kuwaitis are freed from some of their responsibilities in that respect. This fact, observers say, was in part the cause of the economic crisis caused by the collapse of the Souq Al Manakh.[3] They explain it as an example of Kuwaiti eagerness to gain quick profits without serious dedication. This is not entirely true, as many Kuwaitis have entered banking and been successful without depending on immigrant staff.

The real issue here is not the position of one individual in a wealthy country but the placement of each individual to the economic and social benefit of the whole country.

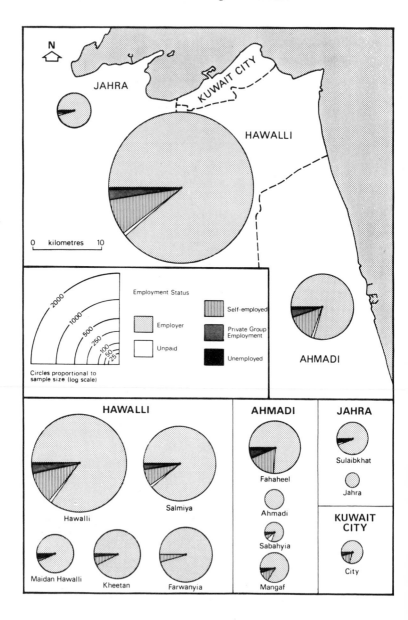

Figure 3.2   Percentage distribution of type of housing occupied by immigrant workers by district

3.4   Housing conditions of immigrant workers

Housing represents one of the major worries among the immigrant population in Kuwait, and also draws a great deal of attention from the government and the Kuwaiti population.

The government concern over the housing problem is two-fold. The first is to separate in location and type Kuwaiti and non-Kuwaiti housing. Besides establishing separate housing areas for Kuwaiti communities, this also involves separation in building types with Kuwaitis inhabiting villas and government housing and immigrants in multi-storey buildings.

The second concern is high housing rents which are continuously increasing due to the new housing rent law explained previously. This law also states that the owner has the right to demolish the building after 25 years. The new law has aggravated the problem still further with the owners usually claiming maximum rent on some properties while rapidly demolishing other houses to establish multi-storey buildings to gain further profits.

Housing, therefore, has created lots of problems and difficulties for both immigrants and government, and is regarded as a valid reason for putting restriction on the inflow of immigrants. Furthermore, it has led to an increase in numbers of immigrants from Korea and the Philippines as these countries provide the construction workforce for basic services which includes housing.

The first aspect of the problem, the separation of the housing for local and immigrant communities in terms of location and type of housing, has in turn created some social and political problems (Al-Moosa 1983) in addition to certain technical and financial difficulties in the services sector.

The first steps of the geographical separation in the housing of the two communities took place by choice at the onset of immigration. At that time, the Kuwaiti population concentration was in the old Kuwait City where the houses were not suitable in quantity or quality to accommodate the large numbers of immigrants. In addition, the Kuwaiti community with its traditional tribal and socio-economic structure was not prepared to intermix with immigrants of different nationalities and ethnic groups.

So immigrants found other localities in which to settle. At first it was in different pockets around Kuwait City, especially in Murgab. With the increase in numbers, they started to live in other areas outside the old city such as Salmiya, Hawalli and Nugra. In the early days these areas were open countryside; places for camping during the spring time; places where some bedouins practised vegetable farming while others manufactured fishing equipment. With the rapid inflow of immigrants and the rising need for more housing, multi-storey buildings containing large numbers of apartments and group accommodation started to appear. This type of housing eventually was to cause the immigrants socio-economic problems.

The new immigrant housing areas were different from the exclusive residential Kuwaiti areas not only by housing type. The immigrants established services in their own areas, such as small shops and restaurants. These expanded with branches in the largest commercial centres of the country in Salmiya, Hawalli, Farwaniya, Kheetan and Fahaheel, a socio-economic distribution not anticipated by the government when it planned the residential layout of the country. Following the government decision to develop the old Kuwait City as the official political, administrative and economic centre, demolition of sections of the old city began. Suitable compensation was given to Kuwaiti house owners and new land was allotted to them outside the city.

Planning was supported by new administrative decisions preventing non-Kuwaitis from buying land.[4] This planning and reorganisation policy was the second channel which deepened the social and geographical isolation between the two communities. It resulted in two distinct groups in the country, one paying the rent and the other owning the houses.

There are strong feelings among many of the expatriate community that legal provision for ownership of their homes by those with long-term residence in the country would achieve a number of objectives not inimical to Kuwaiti prosperity. Given appropriate planning and building regulation controls, the large semi-permanent community[5] could reduce the shortage of housing through their own efforts without affecting the luxury end of the market, where mainly short-stay higher paid professional and technical grades are involved in rentals often at the expense of the government or companies. There would be development (not entirely welcome to all Kuwaiti nationals) of a continuing vested interest in the State by that section of the foreign community which had invested in housing. Activities of this kind that would stabilize the workforce and thereby the foreign population would bring direct economic benefits as households acquired the material possessions and positive attitudes associated with semi-permanent status (IBRD 1965). The process need not be accompanied by alienation of Kuwaiti land if term leaseholds are granted on plots released to this portion of the foreign community. The problem was exacerbated by the fact that the government did not enter the housing market but left it to the private sector which regarded it as a golden opportunity for investments in a country lacking other profitable investment sectors.

In this respect, the total annual rents paid by the immigrants in the early 1980s to the Kuwaiti landlords was almost KD50 million (Al-Moosa 1983, p. 3), accounting for 58 per cent of immigrant expenditures in the Kuwaiti markets. This shows clearly the importance of investment in immigrant housing to the Kuwaiti landlord, especially compared to investments in shares and real estate. This vast sum, no doubt, had negative effects on the immigrants' savings targets, the sole reason for their immigration. High rents made it necessary for some immigrants who came on a contractual basis, such as teachers and doctors, to demand free housing. The same pattern of demands was observed in the contracts in the private sector. This in turn led to a high demand on houses adding a new dimension to the problem. The levels of housing rents had a profound effect on the low-income immigrant families who either left the country or tried to live in collective households. Some worked in more than one job in an attempt to cover the increasing expenses and placed themselves in danger of deportation, as this is contrary to the law.

All this puts the immigrants under continuous pressure facing service expenses such as education and medicine in addition to housing. Such situations tend to maximize the number of males among the immigrants and minimize the number of females. The immigrants who came hoping eventually to bring their families abandoned the idea due to the difficulties of housing expenses. On the other hand, those who came with their families sent them back and lived in collective accommodation in order to increase their savings before returning home.

The flourishing economic period and the establishment of the Gulf shareholding companies that followed the increase in the oil prices beginning in 1973, has helped in pumping large amounts of money into the Kuwait market. This resulted in the inflow of an immigrant workforce in large numbers and a need to provide them with all basic services. Strange anomalies occurred such as a member of a company receiving KD500 as a monthly salary and free housing which cost his company KD700. This factor led to further inflation in house rents and a rapid increase in the price of building materials and the wages of construction workers. The cost of construction of an average house increased from KD30,000 to more than KD80,000, while the wage of a construction worker increased from KD3 to more than KD10 per day.

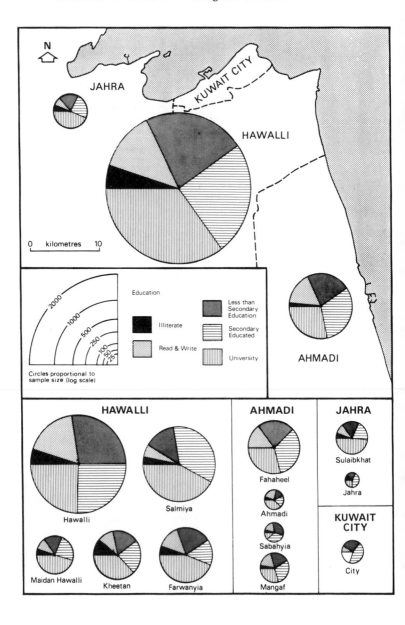

Figure 3.3   Percentage distribution of rents paid by immigrant workers by district

While the labourers' wages increased by 30 per cent during the last ten years, housing rents showed a 100 per cent increase for old property and 300 per cent for new property. This study showed that the average monthly income of a family is KD477, while housing rent is KD100. In other words, the housing rent costs more than the 20 per cent of income which is the maximum recommended by the United Nations. For the majority of families, housing rents are paid from their income and not by their employers. In this respect, our study showed that 89.3 per cent of the sample paid their housing rents directly from their wage earnings (Table 27).

By comparison, the bachelors' housing system gives a different picture from that observed for families. Bachelor immigrants usually live more economically in collective housing, each individual paying a small share of the rent, but at the expense of their health and social standards. A study conducted by the Ministry of Planning describes bachelors' housing to be below the standards recommended by the United Nations Organization (Ministry of Planning, April 1982). It showed that 59.8 per cent of their houses are traditional oriental style composed of a large open area surrounded by living-rooms and one or two kitchens and bathrooms. These houses accommodate about 63 per cent of the immigrant bachelors. Villas, some 3 per cent of the housing stock, accommodate 3.1 per cent of these bachelors while another 3.1 per cent live in single rooms in separate houses (4.9 per cent of the housing stock) and 21.3 per cent live in apartments. 35 per cent of the immigrant bachelors live in houses provided by employers, including 6 per cent accommodated in villas at the expense of their employer. Over half of the immigrant bachelors pay 5 per cent or less of their income on rent while only 5 per cent pay 15 per cent or more of their income. As mentioned earlier, the social dimension of the housing factor stems from a separation of immigrant and local population housing regarding both geography and type.

The original geographical separation came into existence due to the wishes of the local people and the limitation of accommodation in Kuwait City and culminated in the existing administrative system governing real estate ownership. The geographical separation of the two distinct housing types resulted in the social isolation of the immigrants from the local population of the country. Although communication is necessary on a day-to-day basis between the two communities, social and geographical separation is growing.

Some studies (Salem and Addaher 1980) show that the separation is increasing with time. This fact is supported by some immigrants who

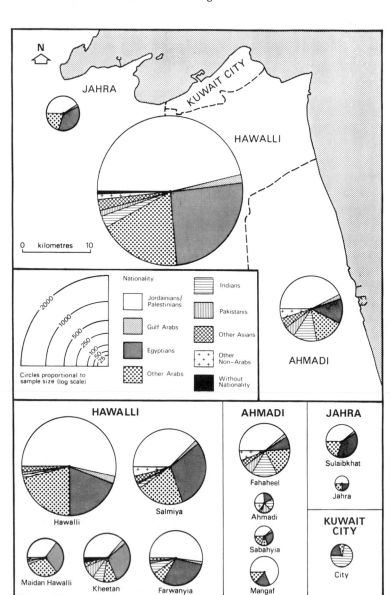

Figure 3.4   Percentage distribution of family size of immigrant workers by district

have been in Kuwait previously and recently returned. They noticed an increase in separation between immigrants and the local people, especially in the settlement areas.

Among Kuwaitis there are varied economic standards concerning housing. In this respect, high-level income Kuwaitis are settled in villas while those with low incomes occupy government limited-income houses of standard design. The high-income houses are usually nearer the capital city. Immigrant housing varies. In one settlement area, some live in large buildings with beautiful apartments costing more than KD1,000 monthly, while in the same area are buildings where apartments are rented at only KD50. There are areas known to have high building standards such as in eastern Kuwait, along the coast and at Benied Al-Oar. Also, large areas of high quality accommodation are found in Hawalli and Salmiya replacing the old houses demolished to allow redevelopment. A number of areas are less well provided for than others, including both the Kuwaiti-without-nationality settlements and the lower-income foreign housing districts (Al-Moosa 1982). There are perceptible differences in the visual qualities of the various housing areas, with the districts occupied by lower-paid foreigners distinctively poorer than others. Parts of Hawalli, where the older properties are rented by Palestinians and others, is a case in point in contrast to neighbouring Jabriya of Kuwaiti and higher-paid Kuwaiti/non-Kuwaiti groups. Urban renewal in Hawalli has merely led to the growth of new semi-slum settlements as its residents move in relatively clustered groups elsewhere.

Immigrant populations are found in nearly all residential settlements, some being designated as non-Kuwaiti areas. Although there are no areas occupied by particular nationalities, various areas are, however, characterized by different types of houses. Moreover, certain nationalities are characterized by certain types of houses too. For example, Egyptians, who are usually engaged in medicine, engineering and teaching occupy better houses and pay an average monthly rental of KD99.4, while Palestinians pay on average KD78.2 monthly, Indians and Pakistanis KD128.5 and KD85.3 monthly, respectively. The highest average rent is paid by the Europeans, amounting to KD150 (Table 28).

Obviously, incomes are reflected in the living standards of these immigrants. The study shows that the crowding levels go in accordance with income too. In this respect, the highest housing densities are among Palestinians, with 2.6 persons per room, while the lowest level is observed among the Europeans, with 0.93 persons per room. The

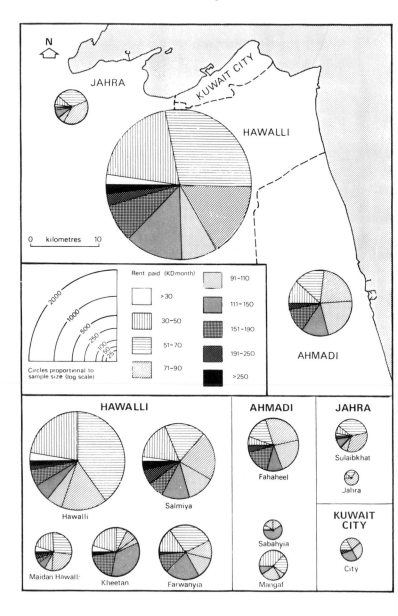

Figure 3.5   Percentage distribution of immigrant workers by numbers of residents per room and by district

Indians, Egyptians and Pakistanis lie between these two extremes (Table 29).

The number of individuals per room is also governed by the household size. Regarding this size of household, Palestinians show the largest amounting to 6.4 individuals, followed by Pakistanis (4.7), Egyptians (4.3) and Indians (3.9), while Europeans form the smallest households of 3.6 individuals. The average size recorded for the private household in 1980 was 5 individuals.

The majority of immigrant households depend on renting accommodation in the Kuwait market and paying rents from their incomes, comprising 89.3 per cent of the total sample. The assumption that the government, which is the main employer in the country, provides its employees with free accommodation is incorrect, as the government provides housing only in a few cases and to a limited number of employees who are brought through external contracts, such as teachers, university professors, doctors and consultants. This fact also applies in the private sector, where our study showed that 71.4 per cent of the Europeans are provided with free housing, 21.7 per cent of the Egyptians and 24 per cent of the Pakistanis (Table 27).

Free housing as provided by employers is of two types. The first category is represented by the consultants and university professors, where free accommodation is part of the work contract and is not linked to other payments. This type of free housing is also found among high-level staff in the private companies and establishments. The other category of free housing is found among teachers and doctors where a portion of their income is deducted as payment for housing.

In the end, the housing problem is becoming a continuous headache for both immigrants and government officials. Moreover, it is adversely affecting the direction of immigration, its composition and characteristics. The problem is rapidly worsening as the provision of housing is left to the private market which handles the problem on an individual basis without any forward plan. This problem ought to be tackled by specialists and plans prepared to alleviate the pressure.

The effect of the problem has been to extend the economic and social problems which divide the two communities. One can understand the size of the problem through the eyes of the immigrants, who feel that they are isolated and wish to use house ownership to solve the problem. From the Kuwaiti point of view, the housing problem is drastically influencing the size, nature and the composition of the foreign labour immigration, a factor vital to the development of the country.

3.5   Social variables affecting immigrant labour

Much discussion is currently being centred on the issue of the foreign labour force in Kuwait. Some leads to a radical view, stating that the foreign labour force will determine the future well-being of the country (Ministry of Planning 1983), while others blame most of the social, economic and political problems on these immigrants. The major factors affecting the stability of the foreign labour force and optimum ways of utilizing this labour have been discussed elsewhere (Al-Moosa 1983). Here attempts will be made to throw some light on the immigration laws, rules and regulations to see how they affect this portion of the population.

There are two important aspects. One is the process of naturalization of the foreign labour force and their long residence in the country, and the other aspect is wages, which is dealt with later.

All research studies and plans conducted so far have shown that the Kuwaiti economy will continue to be dependent on the foreign workforce and that this workforce will always outnumber the local workforce. This study has shown that the shortage in the Kuwaiti labour force is in both quantity and quality, and that shortage in quality is the more serious trait. This is due, among other factors, to the adopted expenditure and development policies. An example of this is the present expansion policy in the health services, which resulted in the opening of three large hospitals, in a very short period, all equipped with sophisticated and expensive medical equipment. This sudden expansion was undertaken at a time when the Ministry suffered from a shortage of doctors and skilled technicians. This shortage is reflected in the Ministry's policy which prevents any doctor from practising his profession outside government hospitals and clinics. Such rules applied not only to foreign doctors, but to Kuwaiti doctors too. Similar policies are also applied in educational and other services.

The question always raised is, for which community is the planning done, for Kuwaitis alone or for the whole population in Kuwait? There is no declared policy, but the government is planning for two communities; one immigrant and the other local. Although all the national plans are different in their approach and methodology, they all assume the existence of two communities. Moreover, these plans have always been oriented towards meeting certain needs and expectations over a limited time span. The first plan prepared by Sir Colin Buchanan was based on certain assumptions regarding the volumes and rates of immigration, while the second amended plan presented by Shankland Cox was based on the hypothesis that the rate of immigration is dependent on shortage in the local labour force. Such planning practice is clear in all sectors of the economy. For example, the volume and quality of imports cannot only be oriented for Kuwaitis. The same applies in planning for the services sector, especially in housing where 60 per cent of the houses are occupied by non-Kuwaitis. In educational sectors 50 per cent of students are immigrants and in the health service 66 per cent of the registered patients in 1981 (Statistical Abstract 1982, Vol. 19) were immigrants. The expansion in roads and flyovers took into account the immigrants who add extra pressure by using private cars or public transport. In this respect, the mileage of all-weather roads rose from 330 km in 1957 to 2,729 km in 1980. Obviously, the government planning must consider the whole population.

Plans should concentrate on the optimum volume of immigrant workforce and its rate of growth which will be necessary to sustain the country's economic development. While the rate of growth is easy to determine for the national population, obtaining forecasts for immigrant populations over even short periods of time is very complicated.

Scientific and technological progress has changed the nations' requirements from a quantitative to a qualitative demand. Kuwait, with its economic and natural resources, can do the same for its human resources by training and developing them to be capable of carrying out the country's development plans. In Kuwait too much emphasis is placed on the foreign labour force when dealing with development issues, the local labour force being neglected instead of developed to face the problem. The Kuwaitization process took place in the upper levels of the administrative hierarchy, while professional and technical posts were left for foreign immigrants. The replacement process in these categories is still lagging behind, while real production is in the hands of the immigrant labour force, a situation for which they are not always adequately qualified. The replacement process is to be considered a top priority in order to put productivity into the hands of the local labour force and then plan the role of the foreign force in the country's economy.

The naturalization laws are very strict. Bearing in mind the high proportion of non-nationals in the country and the many sectors in which they are discriminated against, it is not surprising that many wish to become Kuwaiti citizens. The laws do not make this other than almost impossible and the numbers quoted as receiving this highly sought condition are most likely to be bedouin, not non-Kuwaitis (Farah, al-Salem and al-Salem 1983).

It is true that Kuwait, with its harsh climate and dry lands together with its limited investment markets, is not a place to attract immigrants. Other than the availability of jobs, there is no logical reason for immigrants to come. In the period prior to the oil discovery no immigrants came other than from those countries which had a strong 'push' factor.

The issue of immigration should be tackled with care. In a country where immigrants constitute 60 per cent of the population and affect all its economic and political aspects, long-term plans should be prepared to cover all possible factors.

A large portion of Kuwaiti investors are dependent on the immigrant housing sector, while the Kuwaiti consumer market depends on the immigrants too. In addition, administrators at all levels have benefited from the existence of the foreign labour force in the government and private sector, and are dependent on immigrant labourers, who, unlike the Kuwaitis, never come into conflict with their supervisors. On the other hand, the foreign employees try to obtain situations at work which are unrelated to their skills, often causing a deterioration in work standards and productivity. The outcome of such a situation is to label both employer and employee as unproductive.

In a study on productivity deterioration of the Egyptian workers in the Gulf, Dr Saed Al-Dien Ibrahim states (Ibrahim 1982, p. 137) that in many cases they stop self-education and neglect to improve their work performance even in cases where their qualifications and skills match the official job description they are occupying. They discover that the real job requirement is below what they expected, especially in regard to performance, which in turn leads in the end to reduction of productivity and continuous deterioration of work. This is true, for example, in cases of university professors. Although the rich Arab countries of the Gulf recruited the best professors from Egypt, Lebanon and Syria, these professors were given a very low teaching programme of 6 to 9 hours weekly, for a tenfold increase in salary.

Unfortunately, this decreased their productivity, especially in situations where remuneration or contract renewal are not geared to an improvement in work performance and work competition. Another problem related to the immigrant labour force is the dependence on foreign experts and consultants to the exclusion of Kuwaitis. This practice is as wasteful as it is unfortunate, as the Kuwaiti consultants have, in addition to their skills, a knowledge of their home environment so are as well qualified to give the right solutions to their country's problems. Such situations create misunderstanding and friction between Kuwaitis and immigrants. The bitterness in the immigrant which results from his knowledge that his stay in the country or progress in work is dependent on the satisfaction of his Kuwaiti superiors, can be overcome by granting long-term residence visas to those with a good record and productive performance.

Also, payment of equal wages for similar jobs would be very important in improving the Kuwaiti/immigrant relationship and, in addition, may lead to a solution to the service problems especially regarding education and housing. See Section 4.1 for details of immigrants' wages.

The many nationalities and cultures represented by immigrants induce certain social problems. There are two major groupings of nationalities in Kuwait, namely, the non-Arab and Arab immigrants. Arabs constitute a large majority. The blanket use of the term 'immigrants' to include the Arab nationals has created uneasiness and sensitivity among Kuwaitis and Arabs. In order to avoid a feeling of discrimination among the Arabs, another term, 'expatriates', is sometimes used to describe the Arab immigrants, while the terms Kuwaiti and non-Kuwaiti are used in official transactions.

At the start of immigration, Iranians, Indians and Pakistanis constituted the majority among the non-Arab immigrants, these three nationalities having historical, geographical and political relations with the Kuwaiti community. With the increase in other non-Arab immigrants and the inflow of other nationalities such as Filipinos and Koreans, the above-mentioned three nationalities lost their unique situation in the country.

Arab immigrants have advantages over non-Arabs, as their children have rights to enrol in all stages of education including the University, this being because of the shared language. In addition, their priority for recruitment in different jobs follows that of the Kuwaitis, and these privileges encouraged some of the Arab immigrants to enter private business. However, with the inflow of the 'yellow Asians' the whole issue of immigration took on a new dimension, for these newcomers have no historical or social relationships with the community. Males, it will be recalled, are usually found in construction and building, while the females work as maids and in housekeeping jobs. This distribution causes an undesirable social division for, while the males undergo a social isolation as they live in remote and isolated areas, the females live with Kuwaitis in their houses and share with them their social lives.

In Kuwait, as in other Gulf countries, immigration constitutes a permanent problem which results from the diversity of characteristics and social habits different from those that prevail in the host countries.

Kuwait, with its inherited social and economic characteristics, will be unable to absorb such different habits introduced by these newcomers until a lot of work is done to accommodate and organise the immigration process, especially as immigrants outnumber the local population.

The first step in this should be adoption of economic planning which takes into consideration factors of productivity in work. At the same time, this should be accompanied by a parallel effort to change the professional structure of the local Kuwaiti workforce in order to meet the economic requirements of the country. This, of course, should also be preceded by re-planning of economic development to encompass the abilities of the local labour force. Thus, the issue of immigration is to be considered not only from its human dimension, but also from the productivity side.

The issues of naturalization and residence, which are strongly linked to immigrants' worries regarding wages and *Kafeel*[6] for residence and work problems, ought to be tackled with a more practical approach.

3.6   Egyptian immigrants in Kuwait and in Egypt

One of the objectives of the study was to examine the influence of migration to Kuwait by the unaccompanied labour force on those who were left behind. That is, through tracing these families in their home countries and obtaining their attitudes towards the migration of their economic supporters now in Kuwait. The plan of the study was to concentrate on three main groups of immigrants, but eventually, for practical and political reasons, the interviews were restricted to Egyptian families. A number of difficulties were experienced ranging from the unavailability of a representative sample to the reluctance of some immigrants to give permission to meet their families. The majority of the sample were construction labourers and unskilled workers with families, often living in remote provinces beyond the capabilities of this study. For the above reasons, the sample was restricted to the metropolitan areas of Cairo and Alexandria, the sample being 64 families representing the dependants of individual immigrants in Kuwait.

Egyptian emigration to Kuwait is part of the general immigration pattern in the Gulf, Kuwait having known Egyptians prior to the oil discoveries when they came earlier as part of Egyptian educational assistance programmes. Egypt has the largest, the most qualified and skilled manpower among the Arab countries. Additionally, Egypt receives numerous Arab students for university education. Until the end of the 1960s, university graduates in most of the Arab countries and especially in the Gulf states were graduates of Egyptian universities.

Until the end of the 1960s, the majority of the Egyptian emigrants to Kuwait were concentrated in professional and technical jobs such as doctors, schoolteachers and engineers. Even today, they comprise the majority engaged in these professions. Later, they entered other fields, especially building and construction, a major shift in the sectoral distribution of the Egyptian labour force. Of all the Arab immigrants, Egyptians play the most effective role in the country's economy and society. Because of her position as the largest, most powerful, and culturally and politically most influential of the Arab states, Egypt plays an effective economic and social role in all Arab countries, especially in the Gulf states.

Egypt suffers from great population pressure with densities reaching 23,688 persons per km^2, among the highest in the world. In 1976 the labour force in Egypt reached 11 million, which is larger than the total populations of Saudi Arabia, United Arab Emirates, Qatar, Bahrain, Kuwait and Oman together. This labour force is 91 per cent male, the high illiteracy rates among the females restricting their contribution to economic activities. The per capita income in Egypt, regarded as the lowest among the Arab countries, amounted to $320 in 1977 compared to $17,000 in Kuwait and $15,000 in the United Arab Emirates (World Development Report 1983, pp. 148-9). This difficult economic situation in Egypt produced a push force towards other, richer, countries especially the Gulf states. So, the overseas Egyptian immigrant labour force recorded in 1975 amounted to 37,600 in Kuwait, 1,200 in Bahrain, 7,000 in Iraq, 95,000 in Saudi Arabia and 18,000 in the Arab Emirates (World Development Report 1983, pp. 18-23).

During the Abdul-Nasser era, most of the Egyptian emigration into the Gulf area consisted of highly educated and experienced administrators and technicians who usually joined government establishments. Most of these immigrants brought their families with them.

In the early 1970s after Nasser's death, restrictions were removed and the door was opened for emigration, especially towards the rich Gulf states. These Gulf states absorbed immigrant labour into all areas of economic activity and occupations both in the government and private establishments. With these new immigrants, the educational and social characteristics of the Egyptian immigrant workers changed. Accompanied families appeared as well as unskilled workers in the building and construction sector, and the Egyptian workers started for the first time in occupations never practised in the home country.

The new immigrants, making a large Egyptian community, introduced their own social habits. Egyptian restaurants and coffee shops appeared in Kuwait, and unlike the earlier period, the ordinary Egyptian workers in their native dress became a common sight.

The effect of the Egyptian immigration is not restricted to the social and economic aspects of life in Kuwait, but extended to the administrative, legal and the structural formation of different establishments where most of the experts and consultants at all levels were Egyptian nationals.

Until recent years, all the government laws regulating public professions were of Egyptian origin and the educational systems were essentially of Egyptian origin too. Egyptian consultants played a major role in Kuwait, ranging from participation and effective contribution in the preparation of the country's constitution to the establishment of various government establishments. All their activities were confined to the official levels. Egyptian immigrants were not found on any large scale in the commercial activities in the country, so restricting their interaction within the larger community although they represented the second largest Arab group.

A case study on Egyptian immigrants and their families in Egypt

On questioning the families of the immigrant unaccompanied labour force regarding their attitude towards the emigration of their supporters to Kuwait, the majority (89.1 per cent) expressed their satisfaction and acquiescence in current conditions. On the question of the reason for their emigration, 86 per cent looked for improvement of living standards, while 6 per cent concentrated on saving. Low home wages plus their answers above briefly introduce the 'push' and 'pull' factors for Egyptian emigration to Kuwait.

Only a small proportion of the unaccompanied Egyptians (10.9 per cent) stay for periods over 9 years, the majority staying for much shorter periods (Table 30). This is because they usually have only modest objectives to fulfil while in Kuwait. These usually include the establishment in Egypt of a house with all necessary modern electrical equipment. However, on returning to Egypt, difficulties arise which lead to the unhappiness of both the immigrant and his family. 'The life style of Kuwait, with its high living standards is very difficult to achieve in Egypt, so it forces us to stay in Kuwait. Because, even if we transfer home our necessary needs they will be consumed after a while and it will be difficult for us to live without them. This is why we regard getting used to the Kuwait high standard of living a curse as well as a blessing.' In addition, several families of immigrants preferred to return to Egypt since they could not leave their children because of problems with their education.

Some 59 per cent of families expressed reluctance to join their economic supporters in Kuwait. Of these, 11 per cent said the reason was the high cost of living in Kuwait, 32 per cent said they wanted to educate their children at home, 11 per cent gave residence restrictions in Kuwait as a reason, 11 per cent said the reason was the high cost of travelling to Kuwait, while the rest mentioned different reasons such as 'traditions do not allow women to travel', their unwillingness to leave their land and farms, and that the idea of migration did not appeal to them.

In truth, most of these immigrants could not afford to have their families in Kuwait. The majority (80 per cent) earn less than KD400, which is the minimum monthly income permitted by the Interior Ministry (Table 31). Such reasons, therefore, force these immigrants to stay for only short periods. On the other hand, immigrants with high incomes such as doctors, engineers and professors stay for longer periods, even after retirement from their original contracts.

The majority of Egyptian immigrants are highly qualified, representing a loss for their home country. In this respect, our study revealed that 37.5 per cent hold university graduate status, 24 per cent hold secondary school certificates and 12.5 per cent are technically qualified (Table 32).

The new Egyptian immigrants, builders and construction workers, amounted in our study to only 12.5 per cent. The majority were professional and technical workers who comprised 44 per cent while clerical and related workers made up 34 per cent (Table 33).

Egypt is losing badly needed qualified and skilled manpower, but some Egyptian writers estimate that the financial transfers from Egyptian immigrants to their homeland exceeds the returns from both the Canal and cotton export shares. Nevertheless, other writers (Abdul Fadeel 1979, p. 34, and Ibrahim 1982, p. 135) see that the emerging consumption patterns will swallow up most of these revenues while the country will still suffer from deterioration in productivity due to that lost manpower.

In the past, when agriculture was the backbone of the socio-economic structure in Egypt, Egyptians were reluctant to leave their lands. This is why they usually claim that their stay will be only for a few years and 'not exceeding half the number of fingers on the hand'. However, when they discover that their life has been totally changed, they find excuses to stay longer.

Socially, Egyptians rarely mix with Kuwaiti or other Arab communities, although they are very helpful and sociable within their own community. In this respect, 50 per cent of our sample explained that they got their jobs through relatives, while only 45 per cent got jobs on their own (Table 34). Also, the Egyptians respect family ties and we found that 64 per cent of the immigrants visit their families in Egypt on an annual basis, while 8 per cent visit their country every two years, and 3 per cent pay visits once every three years (Table 35), and this despite the high air fare.

Egyptian emigration to the Gulf states has had a significant economic effect at both national and family level through the annual transfers of hard currency, in addition to the durable commodities and gifts which are sent or carried back. A family with an overseas supporter is usually well supplied with consumer goods. Other social impact occurs when a family with an outside income buys a new house, a car and other modern equipment, thus creating new consumption and social habits. This leads to more emigration to help families face these new expenses and to support new families who want this exciting and expensive way of life. Much of such migration is towards Kuwait.

The new expenditure habits introduced by the emigrants' families encourage other people to imitate them (Duesenberry 1967) leading to an increase in consumption. This is borne out by Susan Musiya in her study 'Export of Egyptian teachers' (Musiya, S., 1982). Every person has his own expectations of improving his living standards. This explains internal rural to urban migration within all countries and especially in the underdeveloped world. If difficulties are experienced within one country, people tend to leave for another richer area to seek jobs and better incomes. Egypt suffers as her better people leave.

The economic problems of Egypt and low per capita incomes have created a negative impact on the individual habits and attitudes towards work. A new country gives enhanced opportunities and this explains why most emigrants change their occupation when arriving in Kuwait. In our study, 59.5 per cent of the sample changed their occupations. In the sample, 37.5 per cent were professional and technical workers at home, while in Kuwait their share increased to 43.8 per cent. In clerical and related workers the sample showed that 12.5 per cent were engaged in this profession in Egypt and 34.5 per cent in Kuwait. In agriculture, which represents a major sector in Egypt from which Kuwait was expected to benefit, the number decreased from 6.3 per cent in Egypt to 1.6 per cent in Kuwait (Table 33).

Our study showed that the majority of immigrants are at their most active age. In this respect, 87.5 per cent of those in professional and technical jobs are in the age group 25 to 49 years, and all those in managerial and administration, in clerical, and in services are between 25 and 44 years (Table 36).

The study also showed that 40 per cent of those who get their job through relatives are professional and technical workers, while 34 per cent of those finding jobs on their own occupy their original professions. This means that the import of the labour force is not governed to any extent by formal agreements between Kuwait and the immigrants' home country, especially the Arab ones.

Dr Abdul-Fadeel states (Abdul-Fadeel 1979, p. 47) that we do not exaggerate if we say migration from the non-oil countries in the 1970s towards the Gulf areas has created silent revolutionary changes in the economies and balance of payments of the labour-exporting countries, such as Egypt, Jordan, South and North Yemen. The income and savings of these immigrants is rapidly becoming a major source of national income and influence within the balance of payments of these countries. Immigrant transfers are becoming indispensable sources of foreign currency, especially since 1974 where in some cases they exceeded the revenues generated by the traditional exports of labour-exporting countries. This led to major structural changes in these economies for which there were no precedents. Also Dr Abdul-Fadeel mentions that the average annual transfer recorded by an individual Egyptian immigrant is $205 per annum (1977) and that the income generated by an individual Egyptian immigrant is used by 5.8 persons in Egypt. If we take the total of Egyptian immigrants in Kuwait (380,000 persons), then 221,000 persons must benefit from the gains made by migrant workers there. In a study on the annual transfer of immigrants conducted by the Central Bank of Kuwait, it was concluded that the remittance of the foreign labour force represented 10 per cent of their annual income.[7]

The study also revealed that the Egyptians transferred less than any other group. Egyptian transfers amount to 6.9 per cent, while the Pakistanis show an amount of 27.2 per cent, which is the highest among the nationals sampled. Transfers include expenditures to help families and relatives, and not necessarily for saving or investment purposes. The decrease in the transfers by Egyptians can be explained by the low exchange rate of the Egyptian pound. On the other hand, a large portion of the Egyptians revealed that these transfers are very small compared to their income, and that 66 per cent of the Egyptians transfer only KD50 every month and that 22 per cent transfer an amount ranging from KD50-69. In comparison, 66 per cent of Egyptians fall in the wage group KD100-299. Most of the Egyptians prefer saving. 31 per cent of the Egyptian immigrants save 30 per cent of their wages while 50 per cent save 20 per cent of their wages. These savings are usually allocated for investment purposes as Egyptians carry with them many different commodities on return home.

Such monetary factors encourage Egyptians to migrate. In addition, the prevailing exchange rates encourage them to stay in Kuwait. For example, an Egyptian professor in Kuwait earns, during the four years of secondment, three times the amount he would have earned working all his life in the Egyptian universities (Ibrahim 1982, p. 115). A construction worker earns a sum which is equivalent to six times what he would receive in Egypt (Ibrahim 1982, p. 126).

We conclude that these immigrations are due in general to the 'pull' factors in Kuwait (availabilities of jobs, high wages), as well as the 'push' factors from Egypt (unemployment, low wages). Egyptian migration to Kuwait is faced by difficulties with both negative and positive outcomes. Dr Abdul Fadeel stresses the burden of the social loss being exerted in the national economy and says that the negative outcomes are excessive and not acceptable. Dr Saad El-Din Ibrahim states that the negative effects on Egyptians is witnessed by a decrease in productivity and new undesirable consumption habits.

Countries importing Egyptian or other foreign labour, like Kuwait, face problems of social impact. While development activities in Kuwait are largely dependent on the foreign labour force, which represents a positive outcome of labour immigration, the negative effects are very serious. In addition to the structural changes in the local labour force and difficulties it faces in being developed while contributing to the development of the national economy, the country's productive capacity is seriously at risk from sudden shortages of foreign labour. Withdrawal of the Egyptian labour force, coming from one of the most educated and skilled Arab countries, would pose a real threat.

If the Egyptian immigrations are well planned and utilized to improve productivity by placing labour in the right occupations, the outcome would be to the benefit of the Kuwaiti economy and would promote its development plans.

Such a policy could be promoted by organising immigration through official channels. This would, no doubt, eliminate the negative aspects of immigration on both sides and would narrow the gap between individual and national needs and expectations on both sides, too.

Notes

1.   The Ministerial decision dated 21 August 1977.
2.   Acceptance is limited to Arab nationals whose duration of residence in the country ranges from 10-15 years on the condition that they work after graduation three years in a government establishment for each year of training.
3.   A private stock exchange which collapsed in 1982 with a residual problem of large-scale indebtedness, *Financial Times*, January 1983.
4.   The housing law of 75, 1979. Only nationals are permitted to own the title of real estate, whether land or housing. Even long-term residents with more than 20 or 25 years spent continually in Kuwait have no access to home ownership.
5.   Only 8 per cent of persons over the age of 24 had been resident in Kuwait for more than 20 years and some 17 per cent for more than 14 years.
6.   *Kafeel* is best translated as 'guardian'. It is used to describe the system under which companies must be 51 per cent owned by Kuwaiti interests.
7.   This figure appears to be a low estimate (see Section 4.3).

References

Abdul-Fadeel, M., *Oil and the Arab Union*, Arabian Unity Study Centre, Beirut, 1979, pp. 34 and 47.

Al-Moosa, A. A., *Issues in Development*, Kazma Co., Kuwait, 1983 (in Arabic).

Al-Moosa, A. A., *Housing and Concept of Planning*, The Anglo-Egyptian Library, Cairo, 1983.

Al-Moosa, A. A., *The Degree of Satisfaction of the Foreign Labour Force in Kuwait*, 1983, p. 3.

Al-Moosa, A. A., *Al askan wa mafhum al takhtit al askani* (Housing and understanding planning housing policy), Kuwait, 1982. This analyses the availability of housing and its facilities by selected areas.

Al-Motawa, I. S. E., and Ibrahim, S., *Immigrant Labour Force – Problems and Policies* – paper for Ministry of Planning, 1983, pp. 7 and 8.

Annual Statistical Abstract, 1981.

Annual Statistical Abstract, 1982, Vol. 19.

Duesenberry, J. S., *Income, Saving and the Theory of Consumer Behaviour*, Harvard University Press, 1967.

Farah, T., al-Salem, F., and al-Salem, M. K., 'Arab Labour Migration: Arab Migrants in Kuwait', in *The Middle East*, ed. Talal Asad and Roger Owen, London, 1983, pp. 42-53.

Ibrahim, S., *The New Arabian Social Systems*, The Arab Union Studies Centre, Beirut, 1982, pp. 115, 126 and 137.

IBRD, 1965, p. 26.

Ministry of Planning, April 1982, Bachelors' Housing Study.

Ministry of Planning, 1983, paper presented by Mr Ahmed Al-Daag.

Musiya, S., *Export of Egyptian Teachers*, quoted in Ibrahim, S., *The New Arabian Social Systems*.

Salem, F., and Addaher, A., *The Labour Force in the Arabian Gulf States*, That Esslasel, Kuwait, 1980.

World Development Report 1983, OUP, London, pp. 148-9. Statistics for Egypt are from *UN Economic Commission for Western Asia* (ECWA), 1981. The IBRD put per capita income in 1981 at $650 for Egypt, $20,000 for Kuwait and $24,660 for the UAE.

4 ECONOMIC FACTORS AFFECTING THE IMMIGRANT WORKFORCE

4.1 Wages of immigrant workers

The overwhelming motivation for the flow of the foreign workforce to Kuwait lies in financial reward. Belief that high wages can be earned in Kuwait, accumulated and repatriated, is the main reason why most workers come to the country. Only a very small proportion of immigrants arrive in Kuwait seeking political asylum *per se*, though there has been historically and there remains a flow of people to Kuwait displaced by upheavals elsewhere in the Middle East region.[1] At the same time, better access to consumer goods, improved health or educational facilities than are available in their home territories might to an extent enhance their wish to enter Kuwait but for the most part are subsidiary to the matter of earnings. It is important, therefore, that this review of factors bearing on the foreign workforce in Kuwait begins with consideration of wages earned by immigrant labour.

Average earnings by heads of households are imperfect guides to the levels of income achieved by immigrants. In our sample, principal occupations as a sole source of income provide the majority of immigrant heads of family (90 per cent) with their personal funds, but the remaining workers enjoy multiple incomes of a significantly higher level. There is a different structure, too, in family incomes. Whereas most heads of household (67 per cent) earn on average less than KD400 per month, less than half of household incomes were below KD400. At the top end of the scale, only a small number of heads of family managed to earn more than KD800 each month (5.3 per cent) against twice that proportion of family incomes (11.5 per cent).

From the outset it will be clear that, other than the one universal truth that all worker immigrants come to and remain in Kuwait for the monetary benefits that it brings, there is great variety in the pattern of occupations and earnings of this group. It is also apparent that there is no single mix of costs or benefits attributable to Kuwait's foreign workforce. Each individual, each family and each community (in so far as such exist on a universal basis) reflects radically different positions that make averages for the group as a whole into tools of a crude and simplistic kind.

The capacity to earn wages is in itself not so important as the opportunity for migrants to maximize their disposable income and in particular to make the greatest savings possible. This requires a combination of relatively high cash wages and low outgoings. The relationship between earnings and expenses has been one that has constantly changed over time. During the survey of 1981 and 1982 there was some evidence to show that rising rents for property was diminishing the potential for savings in a perceptible way for the immigrant community. Family groups were more affected than were bachelors since family accommodation in the form of apartments was most affected by rising rentals. Recognition of the problem by the State was expressed in official provision for rent subsidies for certain categories of workers.

Comparative standing of Kuwait against other regional states in the matter of perceived net gains available for immigrant workers had significance both for the initial attraction of personnel to the country and for the retention of that section of the skilled labour force which was mobile. It has been reported in recent years that Kuwait has offered a less rewarding situation than the United Arab Emirates and that, in consequence, there was movement of selected grades of skilled employees from Kuwait to the UAE.[2] On a larger scale, there was an earlier return migration of Iranian workers during the years 1974 to 1976, when the economic boom in that country induced a number of mobile and mainly bachelor Iranians to go back to their homeland. At that time, the comparative advantage for Iranians to remain in Kuwait was clearly less than that of returning to Iran, much of this advantage being expressed in job opportunities and earning potential as well as natural predilection to be in their own country. How much Kuwaiti wage levels have kept ahead of those prevailing in the countries of origin of migrants is difficult to gauge.[3] Certainly, Kuwait was failing to attract workers of adequate quality after 1981. The survey showed that a fair proportion of workers in Kuwait was undertaking employment for which they had not been entirely qualified.[4] It must be assumed, therefore, that Kuwaiti wages were inadequate to attract appropriately qualified staff.

Among the issues affecting total incomes of individuals that was not dealt with comprehensively by the survey was that of multiple occupations. There was a natural reluctance on the part of respondents to give full answers to questions concerning second and third occupations since this is frowned upon by employers and official entities. Only some ten per cent of immigrants acknowledged earning from sources other than their principal occupation. It is believed that this is a serious under-recording of the position. A very large proportion of immigrant workers have other employment, possibly as much as half the male population in this group being involved. For Kuwait, multiple employment of workers brings mixed benefits. On the other hand, there must be suspicions that several employers get less than full dedication from their workers during normal working hours. Workers conserve their energy for the full spread of their occupations. This applies especially to the government sector. On the other hand, it might be supposed that multiple employment enables Kuwait to make do with less immigrant labour than it might do otherwise. In so far as numbers of workers are kept down, so are overheads of the overall labour force.

Yet there must be reservations on the whole matter of multiple employment. Because there is a legal ban on workers from abroad taking more than one job, there is little or no control on the second, third or other occupations. Quality of staff is not scrutinized. Qualifications for these areas may well be significantly sub-standard. There is, in effect, an area of the so-called 'black economy' in which there is little return by way of taxation or other benefits to Kuwait. There is more than a slight suspicion that the government is given less than full measure from its foreign employees, largely as a result of the effects of multiple employment.

Earnings in 1981

Actual earnings by heads of families in 1981 were generally less than KD400 per month. Indeed, more than two-thirds of immigrant workers who were also heads of households or bachelor status fell into this category. Very significant numbers of workers (20.5 per cent) earned less than KD300 per month, though there were negligible proportions caught in the relatively poor group with wages of less than KD100 per month. In the upper end of the salaries scale, a small immigrant group (5.6 per cent) commanded high average earnings of over KD800 a month. Table 37 shows the spread of monthly incomes of main and other occupations.

Joint family systems, in which income from all earning family members living under the same roof is managed by the head of household, persist among many of the foreign communities in Kuwait, especially among those of Arab origin. In some cases members of the family not under the same roof may contribute to the welfare of the parental household, where this is necessary. In consequence, the structure of income for those with their families in Kuwait is essentially different from those living as bachelors. The contrast emerges from comparison between Tables 37 and 38. The spread of income is, predictably, wider for total family income. Only a small proportion of families earn jointly less than KD100 per month and almost two-thirds of families have an income of between KD200 and KD600 per month. At the upper end of the wage spectrum, 11.5 per cent of families earned more than KD800 in contrast to the 5.6 per cent of heads of household in that bracket.

Table 37   Distribution of monthly income from main and other occupations of heads of households (KD/%)

Less than 100	100-199	200-299	300-399	400-499	500-599	600-699	700-799	800 or more
4.1	16.4	25.3	21.5	13.4	7.3	3.3	3.1	5.6

Source: Sample Survey 1981.

Table 38   Distribution of monthly income from main and other occupations of joint family units (KD/%)

Less than 100	100-199	200-299	300-399	400-499	500-599	600-699	700-799	800-899	900-999	1,000 or more
0.2	5.6	17.7	22.1	17.9	13.9	7.4	3.7	2.7	2.3	6.5

Source: Sample Survey 1981.

There is a closer correlation between income levels and family earnings than is at first apparent. Under Kuwaiti laws that govern the flow of immigrant labour into the country it is provided that persons (by definition almost exclusively males) may bring in their families only where their monthly income is greater than KD400 per month. The figure is adjusted from time to time to cater for changes resulting in earning power of the Kuwaiti Dinar. An inbuilt bias of this law is that only the more educated persons bring in their families, the latter tending, by and large, to be themselves in the higher educational grades and so more prone to be employable. The gap between bachelor incomes and family incomes is heightened by this effect brought on as the unintentional by-product of the law. Joint family income is widespread among the immigrant communities, being especially prevalent in Arab, Indian subcontinental and other Asian groups. Joint family income in the full sense of the term is missing only in European families and higher educated groups from other areas where a measure of Westernisation has taken place and small nuclear families predominate.

Educational status was also influential in respect of the earning power among some immigrant groups. The extreme position was illustrated by illiterates, whose range of wages lay between less than KD100 per month and less than KD600. No less than 66 per cent reported that their wages averaged less than KD200 (Table 39). Differentiation between those with primary and secondary education was only slight, suggesting that the foreign workforce was being used in a way that did not discriminate in favour of qualifications and established skills. University graduates and equivalent were heavily represented in the higher income groups, with almost one-third of the total taking more than KD500 per month. Yet it was also apparent that a large number of graduates was prepared to work in Kuwait for modest wages, with 28 per cent receiving less than KD300 per month. Highly qualified personnel in Kuwait appear to form a distinct group within the labour force and are well rewarded. This applies especially to the graduates but, possibly reflecting the value of experience, is also a feature of both secondary and even primary school educated personnel.

Effects of length of stay on income were mixed. Short-stay workers tended to be clustered in the low-wage groups. This indicated that a number of bachelors came for brief residence in Kuwait for relatively low wages. Otherwise, there was a general tendency for the longer-remaining workers to be better rewarded. Though this was far from universally true, it was significant that some 52 per cent of total personnel had been resident in Kuwait for 15 years or more. The short-stay workers were in a minority (15 per cent of the total). Table 40 shows the distribution of income by length of stay in Kuwait.

Indicative perhaps of flexibility in the workforce, but more probably on the basis of the general evidence available a function of the use of the foreign workforce as a utility input, there were twice as many persons who changed from the original occupation they had in their home countries than retained employment within their previous range of skills. Those that changed their areas of employment in Kuwait earned rewards very little different from those that did not.

Structure of the labour force

The structure of the immigrant worker population by age was reflective of the long history of Kuwait as an employer of foreign labour. It must be recalled that Kuwait began to take in large numbers of foreigners as part of the creation of the oil industry after 1951 and, thereafter, in response to the opportunities for development activities made possible by the inflow of oil income. While there is a minor concentration of than the top margin.

Table 39   Monthly income by educational status (KD/% distribution)

	Less than 100	100-199	200-299	300-399	400-499	500-599	600-699	700-799	More than 800	Total number of respondents
Illiterate	31.1	35.0	23.0	5.4	4.1	1.4	. . .	. . .	. . .	74
Read and write	10.0	17.6	33.4	15.8	10.4	5.0	3.3	4.1	1.4	221
Primary school	4.2	18.2	27.2	21.1	14.8	8.4	0.8	2.1	3.2	379
Secondary and above	1.4	21.9	27.3	25.6	9.9	6.0	1.4	2.3	4.2	433
Graduate and postgraduate	0.4	8.2	19.8	22.7	17.5	9.1	7.2	4.4	10.7	571
Total	4.1	16.4	25.3	21.5	13.4	7.3	3.3	3.1	5.6	1678

Table 40   Monthly income by length of stay (KD/% distribution)

	Less than 100	100-199	200-299	300-399	400-499	500-599	600-699	700-799	More than 800
Less than 5 years	13.6	21.6	20.4	11.2	12.8	6.4	2.4	4.4	7.2
5 to 9 years	3.3	15.5	29.7	22.0	13.5	6.9	3.9	2.6	2.6
10 to 14 years	5.1	17.8	21.7	25.4	9.1	4.7	6.3	3.2	6.7
15 years and more	1.4	14.9	26.3	23.1	14.7	8.4	2.4	2.9	5.9
Total	4.1	16.5	25.2	21.5	13.4	7.3	3.3	3.1	5.6

Table 41   Distribution of monthly income of the head of household from main and other occupations by age group (KD/%)

Age group	Less than 100	100-199	200-299	300-399	400-499	500-599	600-699	700-799	800 or more
Less than 30 years	14.5	31.7	26.1	13.2	1.6	1.3	0.3	1.3	1.0
30 to 39 years	1.5	17.1	26.2	21.5	14.2	7.9	2.7	3.2	5.7
40 to 49 years	1.9	8.4	26.0	25.1	13.9	9.4	5.6	2.8	7.3
50 years or more	2.1	13.2	20.7	24.0	14.0	8.7	4.1	5.8	7.4
Total	4.1	16.4	25.3	21.5	13.4	7.3	3.3	3.1	5.6

Source: Sample Survey 1981.

immigrant labour in the younger sections of the population, with 54 per cent of workers under 40 years of age, there is a remarkably large residual sector in the older working age groups. There was a measure of difference between the earning power of the various age groups. Wages of those below 20 years of age clustered in the categories of less than KD200 per month (46 per cent). Workers aged over 40 years tended to fare better than average, falling to a slightly greater extent in the top of the wage range (Table 41).

Whereas the Kuwaiti labour force is serviced by a wide variety of sources, it is Arabs who comprise the overwhelming majority of the workforce. In 1981, approximately 83 per cent of immigrant workers were from the Arab world outside Kuwait. The bulk of the remainder were Asian (9 per cent), mainly from the Indian subcontinent (7 per cent). Distribution of income among the various nationalities showed considerable variety. Among Palestinians and Jordanians, of which the majority by far were of Palestinian origin, there was marked clustering of wages in the KD200-KD400 per month bracket (49 per cent), with only small proportions in the very low and higher levels. The relatively small number of Arabs from other Gulf states tended to be evenly spread across the range of medium to high wage rates. The situation of the Egyptians in Kuwait was very different. Here, the largest proportion of workers was concentrated in the lower categories. More than half of Egyptians in Kuwait take home less than KD300 per month and very few are represented in the higher levels of income.

In the Asian group, the Indians are deeply involved in the lower-paid grades of manual labour and/or clerical jobs, with 56 per cent earning less than KD300 per month and 92 per cent earning less than KD400 per month. The Pakistani community appeared to be generally better off than its Indian counterpart. All those included within the survey had incomes of more than KD100 per month. There were also small numbers who were in the most well-paid bracket. Among the worst-paid groups in Kuwait were Asians from countries other than India and Pakistan. Some 35 per cent earned less than KD100 per month and more than half were paid less than KD300. Other nationalities seemed to be employed mainly in well-paid work. More than half of them earned more than KD600 per month. Whether from Europe, Africa or the Americas, these high earners were mainly in the professional and administrative ranks of foreign employees.

Differentials in wage rates between the public and private sectors were considerable. Higher rates applied in the private sector for those with skills and/or training. Even greater differences were in evidence

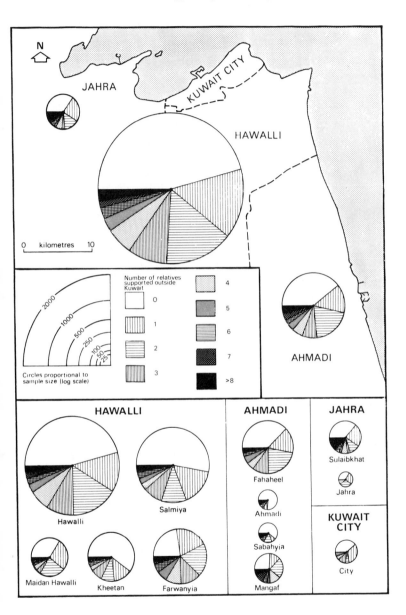

Figure 4.1   Percentage distribution of main monthly income of immigrant workers by district

in the top wage scales, where the private sector often outdid the state sector by a large margin. At the bottom of the range, the state was a better paying employer than the private sector. Almost all employees earning less than KD100 per month were working for companies or private individuals while many of those in the bracket below KD200 were similarly placed. Members of the foreign workforce accrued some welfare benefits but these were entirely non-monetary. There were in Kuwait special arrangements attaching to groups within the foreign workforce where these were brought in under contract from Asian countries. Pakistan, India, Korea and Philippines were the states most affected by this practice. In effect, contractors brought their own workforces into Kuwait for specific projects, housed, fed and paid them almost as external units to the Kuwaiti economy. In a number of cases, payments to workers were made externally, too, with only modest amounts of pocket money made available to them while in Kuwait. This aspect of wage payments was not covered by the basic questionnaire of 1981, which, since it dealt with households, automatically omitted the camps, compounds and special residential sites of bachelor groups of this kind.

A further complication in the situation in Kuwait, though found in other states of the Gulf, was the presence of illegal migrant workers. Living without authority in Kuwait and subject to extradiction if discovered, these workers were open to exploitation by unscrupulous employers. They were often paid very poor wages, had access to none of the Kuwaiti welfare state system, and were poorly housed. Most of the illegal immigrant workers were not documented by the survey of 1981. Estimates of total numbers of illegal workers vary considerably and there is no systematic data available on the wage rates prevailing among them. For working purposes, it was assumed that there were some 40,000-50,000 illegal workers in Kuwait in early 1982.[5]

Geographical distribution of the workforce in Kuwait, as diagnosed by the survey of 1981, showed a marked concentration in Hawalli Mohafeda with 80 per cent of the total. Since there tended to be a correlation between nationality and place of residence, there was also a close link between place of residence and wages earned. The extremely poor areas for wages were Jahra Mohafeda as a whole, together with Kuwait City, Kheetan and Mangaf, where few or no workers were in receipt of wages of more than KD600 per month. This pattern was reinforced by consideration of wage earners with less than KD300 per month, in which Sulaibikhat, with two-thirds of its workforce in this category, was among the poorest rewarded areas of Kuwait. Kheetan,

Hawalli Sabahyia, Farwaniya and Ahmadi all contain working populations of foreigners, more than half of which earn less than KD300 per
month. Mangaf and Kuwait City are little different from other poor
wage group districts.

A clear disparity emerges between the areas already named and those
areas with often sizeable but none the less well-paid foreign communities. The extreme case is illustrated by Maidan Hawalli, where only 28
per cent of the foreign workers earned less than KD300 per month. The
position at Salmiya had similar characteristics, though here with a
rather larger workforce involved, while Fahaheel had only one-third of
its workforce in this category. Full details of the distribution of incomes
by areas of residence are shown in Table 42.

Conclusion

Kuwait has become almost a symbol internationally for its high per
capita income. The International Monetary Fund suggested an average
income in the State of $20,900 in 1981 (World Development Report
1983, World Bank, p. 149). Yet it has been shown in this independent
study that the distribution of incomes has a number of characteristics
that make the average position profoundly misleading. This is especially
so for the foreign workforce.

It is far from straightforward to isolate the variables that play the
greatest role in determining income for non-Kuwaitis. A number of
correlations appear to be strong enough to indicate at least a beginning
for an analysis. However, their social and political implications appear
to offer grounds for disquiet. In particular, there are notable geographical concentrations of specific national groups with low average
wage levels. These same groups tend to have large families and to have
lived in Kuwait often for a prolonged period. Most have little hope of
achieving Kuwaiti nationality under present regulations and with
present attitudes towards them by society at large. Economic survival
for many in this category depends on continuing access to multiple
incomes for the head of household and/or other members of the joint
household.

The utility of the foreign workforce to Kuwait defies quantification
as one might expect. Indeed, the question to a large extent begs the
critical issues. The non-Kuwaiti Arabs form the overwhelmingly important portion of the foreign workforce with approximately 83 per cent
of the total. Many have been resident in Kuwait for so long that they
form an effective part of the domestic labour force although technically
registered as non-Kuwaitis. As part of the total labour force in Kuwait,

Table 42   Total monthly income from main occupation by district (KD/% distribution)

	Less than 100	100-199	200-299	300-399	400-499	500-599	600-699	700-799	More than 800	Total number of respondents
Hawalli										
Hawalli	3.7	18.8	29.1	20.5	11.8	5.6	1.2	3.0	6.3	575
Salmiya	2.6	13.1	17.6	20.1	18.2	7.4	6.5	5.1	9.4	352
Maidan Hawalli	4.7	8.2	15.3	30.7	10.6	8.2	8.2	4.7	9.4	85
Kheetan	7.2	24.5	26.6	15.8	14.4	10.1	...	1.4	...	139
Farwaniya	5.9	16.1	30.7	22.0	12.9	7.5	2.2	1.1	1.6	186
Total Mohafeda Hawalli	4.1	16.8	25.2	20.8	13.8	7.0	3.1	3.2	6.0	1337
Kuwait City										
City	...	16.0	32.0	24.0	16.0	12.0	...	...	...	25
Ahmadi										
Fahaheel	2.5	6.8	23.6	23.6	14.3	12.4	7.5	4.3	5.0	161
Ahmadi	23.7	14.3	14.0	14.3	...	4.8	...	2.8	23.8	21
Sabahyia	8.3	25.0	20.8	29.1	4.2	4.2	4.2	4.2	...	24
Mangaf	4.7	20.8	23.3	23.3	18.6	9.3	...	...	...	43
Total Mohafeda Ahmadi	5.2	11.6	22.5	23.4	12.9	10.4	5.2	3.6	5.2	249
Jahra										
Sulaibikhat	1.8	27.3	38.2	25.5	3.6	...	1.8	...	1.8	55
Jahra	...	25.0	25.0	33.3	16.7	...	...	...	...	12
Total Mohafeda Jahra	1.5	26.9	35.7	26.9	6.0	...	1.5	...	1.5	67
Total All Mohafedat	4.1	16.4	25.3	21.5	13.4	7.3	3.3	3.1	5.6	1678

the non-Kuwaiti Arabs are significantly large with more than 70 per cent. Their presence has become both essential for the running of the State and also self-reinforcing in so far as their long-term demand for goods and services has created its own cycle of activity.

As a result of the difficulties for foreign workers, even if of Arab origin, in taking out Kuwaiti nationality, most foreign workers retained contacts with their home countries and maintained a steady flow of funds from their earnings in Kuwait for remittance to recipient individuals and institutions overseas, in which Jordan, the West Bank of the Jordan and Egypt were the main destinations. Significant volumes of investment and consumption were foregone by Kuwait through the entirely unrestricted transfer of funds from outside the State.

Overall, the survey suggested that wage levels of the foreign workforce were highly variable but tended on average to be modest both in comparison to rates enjoyed by Kuwaiti nationals and those prevailing elsewhere in the Gulf region. But it was also clear that the long-stay nature of Kuwait's foreign, mainly Arab, workers gave stability to the workforce to offset short-term wage effects *vis-à-vis* competitive areas elsewhere in the Gulf. Continuing economic depression as a result of the decline in Kuwaiti oil revenues, growing levels of domestic price inflation and hardening perceptions of alienation could undermine the apparently secure labour force enjoyed by Kuwait in the past.

4.2 Skills of the foreign workforce and the appropriateness of their use

The point has already been made that the foreign workforce in Kuwait tends to be employed in a utility role. This is particularly the case with those not in the two vocationally oriented groups, viz. excluding professional and scientific and agriculture and fisheries. The division also has a certain nationality aspect in so far as those of Arab or Asian origin brought in as individuals tend to be most used in the factotum role. Like European and American workers in Kuwait, those Asians working within labour contract groups tend to be more specialized than the foreign workforce as a whole, since they are brought in to perform specific functions provided for within a fixed contractual framework.

While at first sight there appears to be a close correlation between occupations in Kuwait and those pursued in country of origin, as shown in Tables 21 and 22, the position is rather less clear when looked at from the criterion of the proportion of the group actually following their original occupations in Kuwait. Only 68 per cent of all workers remain with their occupations on arrival in Kuwait, the most marked strand of continuity being the general category of professional and technical workers, where 89 per cent of those surveyed reported being engaged in their principal occupations of their countries of origin. Elsewhere, there was less close linkage between those activities pursued in Kuwait and original occupation. Notably, significant numbers of persons who were labourers in their native countries acted in more elevated positions in Kuwait, while, at the opposite extreme, even larger numbers of former professional and technical staff were apparently prepared to work in lesser occupations in Kuwait (Table 43).

Differences between males and females in occupational status in country of origin were marked. The majority of women in gainful employment in Kuwait came from professional, technical or clerical backgrounds, accounting for almost 90 per cent of the total. Some 62 per cent of males were drawn from these groups, the large discrepancy occasioned by the low numbers of women involved in the labouring group of activities.

The regional distribution of the labour force, as determined by those retaining the same employment in Kuwait as they held in their countries of origin, is only partially illuminating. Not all workers gave full details of their status and in any case the sample numbers in some areas were too small to be of significance. Data in Table 44 indicate none the less that there is a high relative correlation between location and job retention from the state of origin in Hawalli Mohafeda, where 87.8 per cent of the labour force actually pursuing the same employment was to be found. Even in Hawalli, however, only 35.2 per cent of the total labour force was in the same job as had been followed in the country of origin.

In addition to the professional and technical group, there was a marked correlation between those in a specific employment category and retention of the same job. The agriculture and fisheries sector was one such case, where almost 89 per cent of the group were in their original field of employment. There was some tendency, too, for the labouring and production group to stick with its class. Here, some two-thirds of workers in the category were still engaged in manual work of an unskilled kind. But it is remarkable that so many persons were spread across other sectors of activity in areas where they clearly were without training, 6.5 per cent, for example, claiming status as professional and technical grades. A high degree of flexibility affected all other groups, with more than half of all those from any employment category in their home countries used in other categories in Kuwait,

Table 43   Relationship between main occupations in country of origin and Kuwait

Occupation in country of origin	1 Professional + technical No.	%	2 Administrative + managerial No.	%	3 Clerical + executive No.	%	4 Sales No.	%	5 Services No.	%	6 Agriculture + fishing No.	%	7 Production + labouring No.	%	8 Total No.
1 Professional + technical	411	88.7	10	2.2	29	6.3	8	1.7	1	0.2	—	—	4	0.9	463
2 Administrative + managerial	20	45.5	16	36.3	7	15.9	1	2.3	—	—	—	—	—	—	44
3 Clerical + executive	26	20.6	10	7.9	70	55.6	4	3.2	6	4.8	—	—	10	7.8	126
4 Sales	12	15.6	6	7.8	8	10.4	35	45.4	5	6.5	1	1.3	10	13.0	77
5 Services	1	2.2	2	4.4	5	11.1	2	4.4	21	46.8	—	—	14	31.1	45
6 Agriculture + fishing	3	2.8	2	2.0	13	12.7	9	8.8	23	22.6	8	7.8	44	43.2	102
7 Production + labouring	12	6.5	5	2.7	3	1.6	14	7.5	7	3.8	—	—	145	77.9	186
Total	485	46.5	51	4.9	135	12.9	73	7.0	63	6.0	9	0.9	227	21.8	1043

Source: Sample Survey 1981.

though inappropriateness of occupation in Kuwait was less real than apparent since there must be deemed to be a considerable overlap between the groups designated as clerical and executive, sales, and services.

Of those in the same job as in their countries of origin from the accompanied workers group, there was a strong emphasis on the professional and technical grade, with 58 per cent of the total. Only the production and labouring group, with some 21 per cent, approached this level (Table 45).

The distribution of skills of an appropriate kind, as determined by transfer of personnel to Kuwait within the same employment group as in their states of origin, shows a total of 68 per cent of the overall accompanied labour force (Table 45, column 3). A skew towards the professional and technical grades is consistent with other characteristics, while the lower rating of the production and labouring group vis-à-vis the proportion of the total labour force surveyed (i.e. 13.9 per cent against 21.8 per cent) can be dismissed as a gain to Kuwait. Where foreigners are prepared to lower their status (on the assumption of lower wages) then Kuwait receives an improved workforce. It might be argued, however, that providing foreign labour accompanied by families with lower-grade employment than their training indicates probably means that the state is under-utilizing its long-term foreign labour force and possibly overpaying its labouring groups too.

Ultimately, the criteria that apply to the appropriate use of the foreign labour force are not so much internal to that group, but rather derive from the degree to which it is acting as a complement to the indigenous labour force.[6] As part of this consideration, the workers mobilized from outside Kuwait must be seen in two major lights. First, as making good deficiencies in the Kuwaiti employment structure without inhibiting the growth of indigenous skills in those areas fulfilled by the foreigners. Second, as an interim solution seen against a chronology of local development objectives.

It is ironic that the apparently temporary status of the foreign workforce has never been defined in either way if only as a modest beginning to determining its role. Substitution of Kuwaiti for foreign labour was never realistically feasible against the effects of important variables such as indigenous cultural bias against manual occupations, of which much has been made in the literature (Alessa 1981, p. 2). At the same time, the statutory provision of employment for all Kuwaiti nationals has also meant that the civil service has been an attractive source of work for Kuwaitis, since it goes with undemanding conditions in the place of work, together with other generous pension and service rights. Rates of pay in the areas open to government employment for Kuwaitis have tended to be maintained at premiums above those available elsewhere for less onerous conditions. Although the Government of Kuwait has consistently provided excellent educational facilities in the State, Kuwaiti nationals have not come forward in either adequate numbers or across an adequately wide spectrum of subjects to make up a significant factor with which to substitute for any appreciable proportion of the foreign labour force.

Table 44   Retention of same jobs in Kuwait as in country of origin — by district (%)

	1 *Total labour force retaining same job as state of origin*	2 *1 as % of total foreign labour force in same job*	3 *1 as % of district labour force in same job*
Hawalli			
Hawalli	9.1	28.9	28.5
Salmiya	10.6	33.7	47.0
Maidan Hawalli	2.8	8.8	50.9
Kheetan	1.9	6.1	23.7
Farwaniya	3.3	10.3	30.6
Total Mohafeda			
Hawalli	27.7	87.9	35.2
Kuwait City			
City	0.2	0.9	12.5
Total Kuwait City	0.2	0.9	12.5
Ahmadi			
Fahah	0.8	2.5	8.4
Ahmadi	—	—	—
Sabahyia	0.1	0.3	8.3
Mangaf	1.1	3.3	38.3
Total Mohafeda			
Ahmadi	2.2	6.1	13.5
Jahra			
Sulaibikhat	1.4	4.6	36.6
Jahra	0.2	0.6	22.2
Total Mohafeda			
Jahra	1.6	5.2	34.0
Total	31.7	100.0	31.5

Source: Sample Survey 1981.

Structural factors are at work too. Even as early as the 1960s, the United Nations observed that the Kuwaiti population would need to increase rapidly in size merely to replace the then foreign workforce of 122,212 persons. Indeed, it was estimated that it would have taken 40 years simply to achieve that objective (IBRD 1965, p. 26). A rising Kuwaiti population and increased economic expectations have put such a target well beyond reach, even within the span of 40 years since per capita demand for services has grown faster than even a resilient birth rate of population growth (the latter put at 6.3 per cent in 1980) could provide for. Per capita income, an imperfect but useful indicator of the gross demand for goods and services, rose from KD3,220 in 1970 to KD3,500 in 1975 and KD5,440 in 1980.[7] Income of Kuwaiti nationals tended to rise at a rate somewhat above the average for the State as a whole and the scale of growth was perceptibly higher than that suggested by per capita income.

In the matter of official policies towards the development of the indigenous labour force, there has been little serious attempt to rationalise planning of its use on a current basis and even less to elaborate a long-term programme for the comparative contributions of indigenous and foreign workers to the economy (Sirageldin, Lecture, pp. 46-58). The social and economic development plan, 1967/68 to 1971/72, called for a strong push towards lifting the proportion of Kuwaitis in the labour force and also diminishing the numbers of non-Kuwaitis resident in the State as a product of the policy. Under the terms of the 1976/77 to 1981/82 plan, policies were reversed to permit a rapid growth of industries based on employment of foreign workers, including a large number of new immigrants. Rapid change of policy had done little to ensure a smooth and ordered development of the foreign labour force. Meanwhile, acceptance of development projects has not been undertaken with the impact on the foreign labour force as a major consideration, despite the crucial importance of this area to the economic and political development of the State in its broader context. In practice, therefore, the problem of the chronology of change has been ignored in so far as the labour force as a whole is concerned and the structural imbalances between the Kuwaiti and non-Kuwaiti sections of it will persist deep into the future.

Finally, it may be useful to depict the position of foreign labour as self-reinforcing. First and obviously, the foreign element in Kuwait has to be provided with all elements of services and a commensurate physical infrastructure, which itself calls for labour, much provided by the expatriate community. Second, there has grown up a syndrome of dependence by the Kuwaitis on the foreign worker. This appears to affect all levels of society, and culminates in official policies that create the ultimate paradox of pushing for 'diversification' of the domestic economy through adoption of development programmes that are heavily reliant on the import of labour for their implementation. Even where projects are successful, and in the industrial sector in particular there are few schemes that have been readily acknowledged as convincingly viable in an economic sence of being able to survive in parallel with the oil economy, diminution of dependence on a single export commodity appears to be purchased with greater reliance on another externally provided factor, the foreign labour force. Yet this is just as much an area for Kuwaiti concern in achieving genuine and long-lasting domestic development as is the expansion of the non-oil sectors of the economy. Possibly in the longer term Kuwait has a greater need to diminish dependence in its labour supply than in the sources of its national income since the former has far wider social and other implications than the latter. With an oil production/reserves ratio of more than 1:250,[8] the labour problem would seem to be the more pressing of the two. It would not be unreasonable to suggest, too, that diversification itself, though it would to some extent be constrained if foreign labour was available in less abundance, might be more soundly based if it employed Kuwaitis. This would give enterprises the benefit of labour with a strong interest in the economic viability of the concern. Where developments could not be made to run economically with Kuwaiti labour, they could with some realism be ruled out as inappropriate.

Table 45   Aspects of the accompanied foreign labour force — appropriateness of skills (%)

	% distribution of those in same job as state of origin	% of each employment group in same job as state of origin	Number in each employment group as % of total labour force
Professional + technical	58.2	84.7	39.4
Administrative + managerial	2.3	31.4	1.5
Clerical + executive	9.9	51.9	6.7
Sales	5.0	47.9	3.4
Services	3.0	33.3	2.0
Agriculture + fisheries	1.1	88.8	0.8
Production + labouring	20.5	63.9	13.9
Total	100.0	. . . .	67.7

Source: Sample Survey 1981.

There remains, of course, the option for Kuwait to manipulate its labour force by legislation. With particular respect to those included in the survey of 1981, i.e. long-term residents accompanied by their families, a change in the laws of residence and especially nationality would transfer a significant but not overwhelming proportion of the workforce from the non-Kuwaiti to the Kuwaiti side of the equation. Although there have been proposals for an alteration in the nationality laws in Kuwait for many years, progress in this area must be expected to be slow[9] and an immediate solution to the problem might not be found in such an approach.

4.3   Financial transfers by immigrant workers

The volume of financial transfers by immigrant workers to destinations outside Kuwait is not known with certainty. Estimates are included in the assessments of the cost of the immigrant workforce in Sections 4.4 and 5.2 of this volume. The World Bank has also made an evaluation of the flow of remittances abroad of the immigrant workers in Kuwait. In 1980 it was thought that the basic sum involved in such transfers was KD182 million (or $615 million). Yet this, it was admitted, excluded remittances by expatriates for investment purposes and did not take account of the value of goods shipped from Kuwait by foreign workers. There is every reason to believe, too, that the official estimates on which the World Bank made its calculations significantly under-valued transfers. Central Bank of Kuwait figures for financial transfers overseas by non-Kuwaitis are shown in Table 46. It would appear that the total of transfers abroad, including goods bought in Kuwait and other transfers not recorded in official statistics must be in the region of $1 billion each year, much destined for the West Bank territories, Jordan and Egypt. Minor but important flows for the countries concerned are directed to Iraq, Iran, the Indian subcontinent and the Philippines. A portion of funds moved abroad goes to third countries for investment purposes or to pay for the education of children of immigrant workers in Kuwait. Indeed, it is known that agents in Kuwait act as collectors of earnings of immigrants. Such funds are moved abroad to centres such as Geneva while immigrants receive counterpart payments in their home countries, often at a premium rate. In such transactions, the home governments of immigrants are deprived of the foreign exchange value of their immigrants' labour. Seccombe noted that Jordan in the 1970s went out of its way to encourage capital flows from immigrant workers in the Gulf to send home their remittances through official channels through the offer of high exchange rates and grant of permission for workers overseas to keep funds in Jordan in foreign exchange accounts. Special bonds were also issued to give further incentive for funds to return home in areas that could be used for the national benefit (Seccombe 1981, p. 8).

Table 46   Current private transfers abroad by non-Kuwaitis — 1975-1980 (KD/mn)

Year	KD mn
1975	80.0
1976	92.0
1977	106.0
1978	119.0
1979	147.0
1980	182.0

Source: Central Bank of Kuwait, *Quarterly Statistical Bulletins.*

Analysis of the impact of the outflow of revenues from Kuwait is far from straightforward. On the surface, the cost to the Kuwaiti balance of payments from foreign transfers by immigrant workers at a gross figure of, say, KD300 million or one billion dollars each year is significant. It represents, however, only 6 per cent of oil revenues on the basis of 1980 figures issued by the Central Bank of Kuwait (Table 47). While there is no correlation between the two figures, it is an interesting measure that the repatriation of profits from abroad to Kuwait by Kuwaitis has consistently exceeded the remittances sent out of Kuwait by the immigrant workers there.

Part of the difficulty with the remittances sent abroad by immigrants has been the spectre it raises for the future and during hard times. Fluctuations in Kuwait's oil revenues as a result of the poor international market conditions after 1981 and the threat of a measure of financial stringency at home, made the relative foreign exchange costs of the immigrant workforce look more formidable than formerly. There is some justice, also, in the perception that a continuing presence of a large foreign labour force will lead to high future costs on this account. The World Bank, for example, forecast in 1981 that by the year 2000 the foreign workers would be remitting a minimum of one billion dollars each year.[10] Such views of the future tend to be unsettling for Kuwaitis and have tended to colour attitudes to the immigrant workers even at the present time.

Table 47　Balance of payments 1977-1980 (KD million)

Description	1977 Debit	1977 Credit	1978 Debit	1978 Credit	1979 Debit	1979 Credit	1980 Preliminary Debit	1980 Preliminary Credit
1. Goods and Services (Net):		1676		2042		4282		4724
Trade Balance		1383		1625		3660		3740
Exports & Re-exports (fob)		2738		2813		5003		5584
of which: Oil Exports		2504		2584		4703		5187[1]
Imports (fob)	1304		1135		1327		1674	
Nonmonetary Gold	53	2	55	2	19	3	188	18
Services (Net)		293		417		622		984
Freight & Insurance	194	17	181	19	205	28	256	39
Other Transport	39	106	54	111	62	183	77	193
Travel	88	41	106	41	228	97	362	102
Investment Income	57	575	81	815	115	1035	173	1620
Government	(—)	(284)	(—)	(446)	(—)	(532)	(—)	(933)
	(44)	(126)	(67)	(173)	(94)	(243)	(141)	(327)
	(13)	(165)	(14)	(196)	(21)	(260)	(32)	(360)
Other Government	67	11	150	13	110	15	117	34
Other Services	15	3	19	6	20	4	23	4
2. Unrequited Transfers	358		339		356		454	
Private	106		119		147		214	
Official	252		220		209		240	
3. Total Current Account (1+2):		1318		1703		3926		4270
4. Nonmonetary Capital	167		295		130		270	
Direct Investment	35		36			40	118	
Government	(20)		(10)		(12)		(8)	

Table 47   Contd.

Description	1977 Debit	1977 Credit	1978 Debit	1978 Credit	1979 Debit	1979 Credit	1980 Preliminary Debit	1980 Preliminary Credit
Kuwait Fund	(7)		(12)		(6)		(16)	
Other Investment Institutions	(8)		(14)			58	(94)	
Portfolio Investment	45		18		162		89	
Kuwait Fund	(30)			(4)	(47)		(56)	
Investment Institutions	(15)		(22)		(33)		(30)	
Specialized Banks		(—)		(—)	(82)		(3)	
Other Nonmonetary								
Capital	87		241		8		53	
Oil Credit		76	22			53	94	
Government Deposits	56		5		4		50	
Loans	60		90		22			239
Kuwaiti Fund[2]	(55)	(8)	(58)	(9)	(62)	(10)	(88)	(12)
Other Investment Institutions	(50)	(37)	(49)	(8)	(15)	(45)	(5)	(320)
Short-term Capital								
Kuwait Fund	(20)	5	(38)	86	44	(12)	203	
Investment Institutions	(37)	(7)		(38)	(37)	(6)	(193)	(7)
Specialized Banks		(30)	(4)	(80)	(20)		(17)	
Commercial Banks								
Liabilities	52	(25)	210	(10)	(5)	9	143	
Assets	(148)	(96)	(392)	(182)	(193)	(202)	(473)	(330)

Table 47 Contd.

Description	1977		1978		1979		1980 Preliminary	
	Debit	Credit	Debit	Credit	Debit	Credit	Debit	Credit
5. Errors and Omissions[3]		243	744		712		692	
Total (3+4+5)		1394		664		3084		3308
6. Reserves & Related Items (Net):	1394		664		3084		3308	
Central Bank of Kuwait (Assets)	269			116	112		268	
Monetary Gold		(38)						
Reserve Position in IMF		(8)		(41)		(60)		(8)
Other Assets	(315)			(75)	(172)		(276)	
Ministry of Finance	1125		780		2972		3040	

1. Oil exports were valued according to official prices including premiums ranging around 5.5 dollars/barrel applied to a share of oil exports in 1980.

2. Including investment companies and specialized banks.

3. Residue reflecting both errors and omissions and private capital movement not accounted for in banks or investment companies' accounts.

Source: Central Bank of Kuwait, *Quarterly Statistical Bulletin*, Vol. 8, No. 1, Jan.-Mar. 1981.

In the past it might have been arguable that the foreign workforce, for all its problems, did at least ensure the effective running of the national oil industry, which, after all, was the prime earner of Kuwait's foreign exchange income. This is no longer true. Automation of many of the activities in the oilfields and the education of Kuwaitis in the oil industry would permit the running of the sector with only slight assistance from outside and minimum use of foreign labour.

The role of the Palestinian/Jordanian workers in Kuwait is particularly complicated. Most of those falling into this category are semi-permanent residents of Kuwait but have only insecure rights of stay in the State. For many Palestinian families, their children had been born and educated in Kuwait but inherited no rights of citizenship. Given the uncertainties surrounding their position in Kuwait together with their exclusion from ownership of immovable property in the State, this large community acted in the field of remittances exactly as any short-term or bachelor group would have done by transferring abroad significant proportions of their earnings in Kuwait. Exact figures are not known attaching to the value of remittances exported by the Palestinians but informal sources suggest that between one-third to one-half of all remittances from Kuwait are sent by the Palestinian (including those classed as Jordanian) community.

With or without property rights in Kuwait, the Palestinians belong to a greater social entity, now scattered throughout the world as a result of their displacement from their homeland. Their financial responsibilities in this network of national and family allegiances are considerable. Donations are deducted from their State salaries at source to provide an income to the Palestine Liberation Organization. Children under training abroad and scattered fragments of the family in straitened financial circumstances rely on the flow of moneys from their relatives in Kuwait. It is probable, therefore, that the Palestinians would, in any case, be involved fairly heavily in transferring funds abroad even if permanently established in Kuwait with full rights. But the existing situation, in which this group are also obliged to place funds overseas against the day when they run into difficulties in Kuwait or to invest in housing in Jordan or on the West Bank as security for an unsure future, has certainly much exacerbated the problems of remittances by the Palestinians beyond the bounds of a community meeting commitments to kith and kin abroad.

There is a temptation to perceive remittances sent abroad from states such as Kuwait as a form of contribution to regional economic development, as an equalization of income and a transfer of foreign

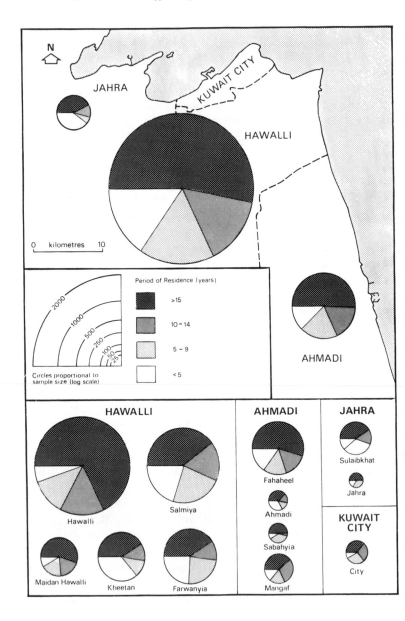

Figure 4.2   Percentage distribution of immigrant workers by dependent relatives outside Kuwait and by district

exchange to more needy recipients. Not all observers accept this view (Birks and Sinclair 1980, p. 103). Remittances tend to fuel inflation in those countries to which large flows are channelled and, far from encouraging productive investment, go towards flagrant aspects of consumption expenditures. In small countries such as Jordan, where remittances have run at more than one-third of Gross National Income in most years since 1976, their distorting effects on other domestic sectors have been profound and damaging (Seccombe 1981). The survey carried out in Egypt during 1983 as a background to this volume indicated similar results even on an economy as large as that of Egypt. At the village level, remittances of migrant workers deeply disturbed the local economy and traditional values within it as funds went into grandiose housing developments, land purchases and marriages (see Section 3.6).

There are a variety of solutions to the problems posed by flows of remittance moneys. A number of countries with large worker populations in the Gulf area have set up banks to enable controlled return transfer of funds and investment opportunities have been made available for individuals in their home countries in ways that are designed to minimize their adverse effects. For the bachelor migrant workers, these are the best means of mitigating the difficulties. Other answers would seem to serve the needs of the long-term residents in Kuwait such as the Palestinians, among which might be the provision of facilities for investments inside Kuwait in areas that would diminish the burden on the Kuwaitis themselves in the provision of housing and services for their workforce.

In reality, mutual suspicions and the inadequacy of the immature financial structures in the Arab world will probably ensure that the present system continues with all its defects. It is not too late for a political solution to the specific Kuwaiti problem of the Palestinian community in its midst, by which a compromise can be effected providing for the accommodation of the long-term residents in secure conditions that include some form of ownership of property inside Kuwait. Events since 1981, in which Kuwaiti insecurity at being a minority in their own land has been allied to falling oil income and a depressed local economy, does not bode well for a settlement, however.

For the future, it must be expected that the external flow of remittances will continue hand in hand with the use of foreign labour. World Bank estimates of transfers for the end of the century, already noted at some one billion dollars, seem high, but indicate a trend that Kuwait appears powerless to influence either for its own or other nations' benefit.

4.4   An assessment of the foreign workforce and its contribution to the Kuwaiti economy

Kuwait is among a tiny minority of states in the world where high standards of living occur propped up by the acquisition of almost all factors of production and consumption from external sources. This has rightly been diagnosed as an historical anomaly (Fergany 1982) that derived from the exploitation of a single asset with special values attaching to it. In other words, Kuwait's virtually total reliance on a single commodity for its wealth has created conditions where a high level of foreign exchange income permits large-scale imports of goods and services, including labour. It might be argued, too, that from the moment that oil revenues began to flow into Kuwait in significant amounts it was inevitable for domestic labour supplies to be exhausted rapidly and for supplementary inputs to be mobilized from external sources. Even modest growth in welfare facilities during the 1950s was enough to outstrip local labour resources. Suggestions that alternative modes of development might have been exploited to avoid over-hasty expansion begs the questions of the local pressures for change, the rulers' wishes to spread the benefits of oil income, and the ruling conventional economic wisdom of that period.

Oil was discovered in commercial quantities in Kuwait in 1938. Serious exploitation began in the 1950s in response to growing world demand for oil and in particular to shortages in the international market arising from the temporary downturn in Iranian oil output, then the most significant in the area. As oil exports expanded and the unit prices paid for oil increased over time, so there was a perceptible and at times, rapid rate of growth in national income.[11] The labour demand of growing domestic expenditures made by the government in particular was met largely by importing workers from abroad.[12] Given the high illiteracy rate in Kuwait at that time (59.7 per cent for the Kuwaitis in 1957), the low availability of skilled workers, with only 14 per cent with an education better than elementary training, and the comparatively low social base of most members of the population, most of whom were previously engaged in trade, agriculture, pearling and marine activities, it was scarcely surprising that there was recourse to foreign labour once the government began augmented expenditures in the domestic economy.

Dependence on foreign workers has persisted to the present time. It is intended here to demonstrate that the foreign labour force has been a vital and mainly majority section of the total workforce. Further, it will be indicated that reliance on this group will not diminish in the immediate future.

It is evident that non-Kuwaitis make up a substantial portion of the population of the State. In 1980 they represented 58.5 per cent of a population of 1,355,827. On the basis of trends established between 1975 and 1980, it is regarded as likely that the foreign population will rise to become close to 65 per cent of the total by 1985 (*Middle East Economic Digest*, 18 February 1983, p. 62). Within the labour force, non-Kuwaitis have greater representation than their relative population size would indicate. In 1980, as noted, the expatriate element of the workforce was 78.6 per cent of the total against 70.9 per cent five years before (Table 48).

Table 48   Foreign workforce as a proportion of the total workforce (%)

Year	1960	1965	1970	1975	1980
	55.0[a]	26.4[b]	57.8[c]	70.9[c]	78.6[c]

Sources: a. IBRD, 1965.
        b. Alessa, 1981.
        c. National Censuses.

The position of the foreign workforce is much enhanced by high participation rates in comparison with the indigenous population. Whereas the foreign workforce returns a participation rate of 47.9, the Kuwaiti group attain only 19.1 (Table 49). Disparity is apparent at all levels. Male Kuwaitis manage a rate of 32.2, only a third of the level of the foreign group. There is an almost negligible participation rate scored by female Kuwaitis (3.2) against non-Kuwaiti females (12.9). Given the large size of the foreign population, the rates result in the Kuwaitis forming a small portion of the workforce. Worse, there appears to be a trend towards a diminution of the Kuwaiti position emerging in the period since 1975. The movements involved are small but perceptible. Kuwaiti males in particular dropped from 35.7 to 32.2 participation over the period 1975-1980. An improvement in the female rate over the same period was inadequate to compensate for the drop and the overall Kuwaiti rate fell by four percentage points.

The position as exemplified by Table 49 has few parallels elsewhere outside the Gulf. Mass flows of labour have taken place in Africa, with the stream of population towards the mining areas, especially in South Africa. West Germany, too, used a foreign workforce to undertake unskilled occupations shunned by the Germans themselves during the period of rapid economic growth up to the early 1970s. In both cases, the availability of foreign workers enabled the economies to run unimpeded by labour shortages during periods of rapid growth, yet left the option of shedding foreign workers when the economy moved into less active phases. Foreign workers were, therefore, used to top up the domestic force when appropriate. Kuwait and other oil-rich states of the Gulf area tend to experience rather different features of their foreign labour forces. Here, the non-national workers form the bulk of the total population and even more substantial portions of the labour force. The foreigners perform a permanent function in keeping all aspects of the economy moving to the extent that they are not expendable except in small numbers at the margin.

Table 49   Labour force by origin and participation rates

	Kuwaitis			Non-Kuwaitis			Total		
	Male	Female	Total	Male	Female	Total	Male	Female	Total
Population (in '000)	278.5	283.6	542.1	497.6	296.2	793.8	776.1	579.7	1,355.8
Labour force (in '000)	89.7	13.8	103.5	332.3	48.3	380.6	422.0	62.1	484.1
Participation rate 1980 (%)	32.2	4.8	19.1	66.8	16.3	47.9	54.4	10.7	35.7
Participation rate 1975 (%)	35.7	3.2	19.5	60.3	12.9	40.7	49.5	7.8	30.6

Source: Sample Census of 1980 and Census of 1975.

Sectoral inputs of the foreign labour force

The importance of the non-Kuwaiti workforce is shown by the sectoral distribution of the total labour force in Table 18. Non-Kuwaitis outnumber Kuwaitis in every sector of the economy. The disparity is greatest in the construction sector, where the ratio between Kuwaitis and non-Kuwaitis was 1:80, a deterioration of fourfold on the position five years earlier. Other areas where indigenous workers were only minimally represented included manufacturing industry (1:12), insurance, banking and financial services (1:4) and transport/communications (1:3).

From Table 18 it is apparent that non-Kuwaitis contribute heavily to all sectors of the State's economy. Indeed, it is self-evident that most parts of the economy would not survive without the input of the foreign workforce. While there is an undeniable correlation between the development programmes and the draw-in of foreign labour to underline such activities as construction and, in recent years, industry, there are considerable elements of the workforce that are required simply to maintain the basic infrastructure, both social and physical, of the country.

The trends in the foreign workforce, especially between the mid-1950s and the present suggest, too, that there has been no substitution function by the indigenous labour force for foreign workers. At the same time, it would seem that there has been no conscious plan by the Kuwaiti authorities to adopt a clear strategy for accelerating this process. In particular, there have been no areas of the economy or the supporting social services where it has been felt desirable to replace foreigners with local workers. All key areas of activity are more or less equally dominated by expatriates. In this equation, there are undoubtedly influences of cultural predilection by the Kuwaitis against certain forms of work, attitudes hardened by economic realities of comfortable, well-paid and socially acceptable employment with the government and its agencies. But the dominating variables would seem to be the twin problems of the nature of the Kuwaiti workforce as defined by quality of skills and its lack of incentive to participate in regular employment, together with the sheer inadequacy of the size of the Kuwaiti labour pool against the claims being made upon it. At the most basic level, the continuing low level of education and training is a severe handicap for Kuwaitis in joining the workforce on an equal basis with foreigners. As late as 1980 the proportion of illiterates among Kuwaitis was officially put at 36 per cent. This situation has become self-sustaining since the Kuwaiti population is not yet producing sufficient teachers and other educators to enable it to become more independent of foreign support. In other words, it is almost as if there was a vicious circle of non-achievement in this critical area.

The foreign worker in the educational system

It is no small paradox that the shortage of trained workers during Kuwait's long period of economic change from the 1950s created a demand for a rapid increase in the educational and training system within the country. The position was made worse by the exponential growth of the indigenous population at rates thought to be among the highest in the world. For many years more than half of the Kuwaiti population has been aged fifteen years or less. Yet the augmenting educational service has been underpinned by the need to import even more workers to staff it. In a situation where reliance on a foreign workforce is translated into a larger and expanding foreign community the dependence on foreign teaching staff will exist for a long time, the Kuwaitis being increasingly unable to make good the many educational defects themselves.

The position of foreign educators has been discussed in Section 3.2.

Foreign technicians and skilled workers

Those general considerations that apply to education as a whole, find reflections elsewhere in the system. Provision of cadres for the secondary and tertiary sectors has probably been more neglected than upper levels of the educational system. Once again, it has to be recognized that there is a universal aversion to manual labour where a better alternative is available. Kuwaitis are no different in this respect from other groups world-wide. There has been a persistent lack of an adequate number of Kuwaitis coming forward for training in technical and vocational grades, since better opportunities are open elsewhere. It is not insignificant also that the structures of the educational system have tended to favour traditional academic virtues. While this has been necessary and could not have been neglected, there would have been benefits in allocating at least a portion of the available trainees to the vocational and technical sectors.

Dependence of Kuwait upon foreign workers is illustrated in Table 18. Most skills are provided by the foreign labour force. In some areas of activity this contribution becomes a virtual monopoly. In the nurses and obstetricians grade, for example, more than 90 per cent of staff come from expatriate sources. General clerking is held 53 per cent by foreigners, though one or two grades here do have substantial numbers of Kuwaitis. The construction industry shows a great concentration of foreign skills, in which the Kuwaitis have little role. Expatriates took 84 per cent of blacksmiths, 94 per cent of carpenters and 91 per cent of plumbers. The oil industry has always been a preserve of foreign workers. Despite various attempts at 'Kuwaitization' this situation has persisted to the present time. In 1980 there was only 36 per cent of the 'mining and quarrying' sector made up of Kuwaitis, though there was slightly more Kuwaiti representation among chemical workers and in the refining group.

The position of the foreign workforce has been sustained despite both the long period in which there has been development of the Kuwaiti portion of the population and the fact that many immigrants bring comparatively low levels of skills with them to Kuwait. The Sample Survey of 1981 showed that a large number of expatriates undertook their occupations in Kuwait as a first job (Table 50). Many expatriates were employed in occupations for which they had little relevant training. Their only qualifications were that they were willing to do jobs that Kuwaitis would not or were not available to undertake.

Table 50   Immigrants taking their first employment in Kuwait

Age Group	Per cent
Less than 30 years	64.0
30-40 years	57.4
41-50 years	59.3
More than 50 years	53.9
Total	58.7

Source: Sample Survey of 1981.

On the supply side, there were a number of training programmes initiated in Kuwait at the vocational and technical level over the recent past. It has been observed however, that many of these were run by different government establishments and were rarely coordinated into an integrated programme (Alessa 1981, p. 111). Experience in Kuwait has shown that the vocational and technical training for Kuwaiti nationals is far from easy to implement. Drop-out rates from such courses are high (Birks and Sinclair 1980, p. 36), with very low motivation demonstrated by students, a situation that appears not to have improved with time. It is likely, therefore, that there will be a continuing dependence on foreign labour across the range of technical skills until both the attitudes towards work in these occupations changes among Kuwaitis and the courses themselves take on a value for them. Changes will have little effect if undertaken in isolation from policies elsewhere in the State, especially those guaranteeing less demanding employment of Kuwaitis in the civil service. It is also the situation that comparative wage rates do not favour the technical sectors of the labour force. To improve wage rates without a certainty that enough Kuwaitis are available or an understanding of the side-effects of an increase in wages in this area on the economy as a whole might be entirely counter-productive.

The foreign workforce – females

For a variety of social reasons Kuwaiti women work only in a limited number of occupations.[13] They are almost unrepresented outside the social service sector and even here there are only small numbers involved in education services and clerical work. The total female Kuwaiti labour force was estimated at 13,829 in the National Sample Survey of 1980 (Table 49), of which 4,851 were in clerical and executive grades and 1,542 in the services sector. No less than 7,190 (52 per cent) were concentrated in teaching, other related activities and general 'professional and technical' branches. There is some truth in the suggestion that segregation within the educational and other social services to preserve a degree of female separateness has exacerbated Kuwaiti problems by requiring the import of labour, a high proportion of it female. Expansion of student numbers or development of the school system has brought with it a demand for more female teachers and ancillary staff to be drawn from abroad or recruited among the existing Egyptian and Palestinian communities within Kuwait.

The non-Kuwaiti contribution to national income

There have been many subjective assessments of the role of the foreign labour force in Kuwait (Alessa 1981; El Mallakh 1979; El Mallakh 1981). Few analyses have attempted to review the situation by purely objective criteria. The present study has enabled the gathering of useful sample-based information on some aspects of the accompanied workforce and it might have value to utilize these data to see if a number of objective criteria may be established. The body of statistical materials available on the Kuwaiti economy has improved considerably over recent years and there are increasing possibilities for making use of national accounts, family consumption budgets and balance of payments figures as a means of testing the role of foreign labour in so far as it contributes to critical economy indicators.

Considerable problems affect assessment of the contribution of the non-Kuwaitis to Gross Domestic Product. Calculation of GDP is acknowledged to be less than satisfactory in Kuwait[14] since a number of variables can only be estimated in an economy that is controlled in part by the private sector and where unofficial trading with foreign countries or unregistered transfers of money in and out the State play such an important role in commercial life. There is a diversity of estimates available. Responsibility inside Kuwait for providing national accounts statistics lies with the Ministry of Planning, though the Central Bank of Kuwait also provides an indicative guide to GDP (*Quarterly Statistical Bulletins*, Central Bank of Kuwait). At the same time, the whole basis of national accounting in countries such as Kuwait has been challenged with a persuasive argument that the contribution of the oil sector has been under-estimated by convention calculation of GDP and its derivatives (*Middle East Economic Survey*, XXIV, No. 47, 1981; MEES 27:4, 1983). For purposes of this review, the figures of the Ministry of Planning have been used as the most recent and best-resourced assessment.

Methodologies available for calculation of contributions by individual sections of the population have been developed for estimation on regional contributions to GDP in a number of countries. The literature on applications of methodologies to situations such as that in Kuwait is rudimentary and even less satisfactory than that available for arriving at, for example, regional GDP. In Kuwait there are particular difficulties since data are far from complete, especially those regarding production and consumption by different economic, ethnic or nationality groups within the State. Similarly, official coverage of the debits incurred by the foreign labour force by way of transfers abroad for funds, gold, or other goods is fragmentary.

Despite the obvious problems involved, it was felt worthwhile to make a general estimate of the performance of the expatriate labour force in GDP if only as a broad guide to the possible scales that prevail. For purposes of clarity, the calculation has been kept as simple as possible.[15] In essence, it has been assumed that the domestic and foreign populations act as an organic whole. The foreign community would be present in Kuwait in only tiny numbers if there had not been the presence and exploitation of crude oil for export. But the oil industry has relied from its inception on foreign labour, materials and expertise for its development and it seems less than realistic to separate off oil as being entirely within the Kuwaiti domain. Recognition of this position is made in the philosophy behind the assessment, though the primacy of Kuwaiti claims on the oil sector is made by beginning with the expatriate contribution to non-oil GDP rather than to GDP as a whole. This has been offset by adding to the base sum for calculation of shares of GDP between Kuwaiti and non-Kuwaiti the expatriate proportion of oil GDP.

The basic equation used is as follows (million dinars):

	Foreign workers'	Transfers abroad by	Share of consumption
GDP:	Non-oil GDP + share in oil GDP	−foreign workers	+ in Kuwait
Contribution of the foreign workforce is approximately	Proportional share in GDP by the foreign workers in the ratio of their participation in the workforce of each sector excluding oil.		

For 1980 application of the formula above would give the following:

Contribution of the foreign workforce is approximately $= \dfrac{2,388.9^a + 3,239.8^c - (420.6^{defg} + 1,791.7^{bh})}{1,361.5 \text{ as per cent total non-oil GDP}}$

$$\dfrac{5,628.7 - 2,212.3}{}$$

" $=$ 56.9%

" $=$ 3,416.4 $\times$ 56.9%

" $=$ KD1,943.9

" $=$ 26.09%

Notes:

a. Estimate of Ministry of Planning, *Quarterly Statistical Bulletin*, Central Bank of Kuwait, Oct.-Dec. 1982, Vol. 9, No. 4.

b. Share of consumption in Kuwait estimated on basis of total foreign population, which was 58.6 per cent of the total at the Census of 1980.

c. The foreign workforce in the oil sector was calculated at some 64 per cent in the Census of 1980.

d. There were an estimated 380,608 foreign workers in Kuwait according to the Census of 1980.

e. It has been assumed that the average annual salary was KD4,418 based on data collected in the Sample Survey of 1981. According to the Results of the Family Budget Survey of 1978-79, Ministry of Planning 1982, average incomes of the expatriate workers were somewhat less.

f. The scale of remittances by foreign workers remains unknown in a definitive sense. Central Bank estimates assume that approximately 10 per cent of income is remitted by immigrants. The Sample Survey of 1981 suggested that higher levels were prevalent throughout the communities, though with significant variations from one group to another. For the calculation above an average remittance of 25 per cent of gross income has been assumed to have been remitted in the form of either cash or kind.

g. Central Bank of Kuwait figures show unrequited transfers from the country by private interests at KS187 million and 'errors and omissions' at KD952 million in the balance of payments for 1980.

h. Total final consumption, government and private, was KD3,057.45 million in 1980, according to Ministry of Planning figures.

Interpretation of the result of the exercise may be deemed to be open to speculation. At face value, the foreign workforce contributed in the region of 26 per cent to total GDP in 1980 on a net basis, i.e. after their consumption in Kuwait and their transfers abroad have been taken into account. It might be deduced that, since the participation is net, the foreign workforce generates one out of every four Kuwaiti Dinars available to the indigenous group. The figures might also suggest that the degree of indispensability of the foreign labour force is of the same order as the minimum cost to Kuwait of doing without its expatriate workers.

At the same time, it is clear that there are substantial costs attributable to the foreign population as a whole in a purely economic arena.

It could be suggested for instance, that for a net gain of 26 per cent of its GDP, the State has to make an initial outlay in domestic currency and foreign exchange costs of some 30 per cent of its GDP. The calculation does, therefore, show up the acute dilemma for Kuwaitis in evaluating the utility of the foreigners inside their country. While there is a very substantial return for their acceptance of the foreign workforce, there are severe financial costs, too, in addition to perceived social and cultural burdens arising from the numerical imbalance between the local and foreign populations.

Foreign exchange costs of the foreign workforce

The question of the effects on the balance of payments of the existence of a large foreign community in Kuwait was rarely pressing as a problem until recent times. There were appreciable falls in the value of income from abroad, that became particularly noticeable from 1982 as both volumes and prices of oil exports fell, with a parallel fall in income from overseas investments as interest rates fell world-wide. At this stage, the foreign exchange costs of the expatriate group began to be taken more seriously.

In fact, the real scale and rate of transfers of funds from Kuwait is not known with certainty. Neither are counter-flows of funds brought in by some of the foreign community for use inside Kuwait. Official estimates suggest that, for working purposes in construction of the balance of payments position of the country, a 10 per cent proportion of the earnings of the foreign community flows out as remittance money to immigrants' families or as investment funds to outside destinations. Respondents in the Sample Survey of 1981, undertaken as part of this research project, indicated that rather larger funds were remitted to their states of origin. While varying, as noted, by nationality, occupation and family status, the proportion of remitted income was more in the range of 15 per cent than 10 per cent. When account is taken of gold (often in the form of jewellery) and other goods transferred out of Kuwait by returning immigrants, it would appear to err on the side of safety, so as not to exaggerate the role of the expatriates, by assuming a 25 per cent rate of transfer of salary from Kuwait.

Salaries in Kuwait are surveyed at the household level (Ministry of Planning, Vol. 9, No. 4, 1982). The Ministry of Planning reported that average monthly incomes of expatriates were some KD190 against KD496 for Kuwaitis. The official survey was implemented with skill, though there were predictable difficulties in obtaining answers to questions concerning income and it would seem unwise to assume that the figures presented accord entirely with reality. Some similar constraints apply to the project survey of 1981 though here the adduced annual average income per head was KD4,418. This accords closely with Central Bank of Kuwait estimates and was therefore used in preference to official data.

In aggregate, the total outflow of funds on account of the foreign population as cash and other transfers was put at KD420.6 million in 1980. This sum exceeded the figure of unrequited transfers used by the Central Bank in its balance of payments estimates since the bank assumed the lower level of income remitted of 10 per cent against 25 per cent taken as the basis for calculations above. There is an assumption, too, that the KD420.6 million was net.

It has been argued that Kuwait gains indirect financial benefits through recruiting its workforce abroad, a system in which other governments and individuals foot the bill for education and training.[16] While there is some truth in this assertion, it must be borne in mind that a large proportion of the foreign workers in Kuwait are in grades of occupation such as labouring and manual workers in production, which require little formal training or education. Meanwhile, an appreciable proportion of the foreign workforce takes up its first job in Kuwait and brings with it no experience gained at the expense of overseas governments.[17]

The foreign labour force as a domestic market

There is strong belief in Kuwait that the merchant class has a strong vested interest in maintaining or even increasing the size of the foreign population as a means of forwarding its commercial interests. The suggestion is that the greater the number of consumers, the greater the market and scope for profit making. The argument merits some attention, partly because it is widely prevalent, and also because there do indeed appear to be a number of factors that support it. To what extent pressure from the merchants is ultimately translated into action by the political authorities in Kuwait is a question that cannot be answered here.

The principal characteristic of the Kuwaiti market is the smallness of its size (Al-Abdul-Razzak, Ph.D unpublished, 1979). By 1980 there were 1,355,827 persons in the State. Of this total, 562,065 were Kuwaitis. In terms of per capita income, Kuwait ranked among the richest in the world with KD5,496 in 1980. Since oil revenues permit, among other things, the import of goods and services, a very high proportion of these are handled by the large trading houses in the State.

The position of control is enhanced by the poverty of domestic productive assets outside the oil sector. Legal constraints on ownership of businesses in Kuwait determine that Kuwaitis retain control, if only in name, of commercial activities, including import and wholesale/retail trade inside Kuwait. Because of the history of Kuwaiti commerce before the dominance of the economy by the oil sector, together with reinforcing political factors, a small number of trading families hold large portions of the market through a combination of their financial resources and ownership of exclusive agencies for handling imported materials. On the surface, at least, the association of factors — high levels of imports, the limited nature of the domestic market as defined by numbers, the strong position in the supply of goods of a number of traditional trading families and the perceived political influence of those same families — there do appear to be *a priori* grounds for suggesting linkages between a desire to expand the domestic market, a requirement to achieve that by permitting growth of the immigrant sector and maximization of the profits of all Kuwaitis involved in commerce.

In practice, the correlations are slightly less strong than sentiments on the issue suggest. In view of the high levels of remittances for the majority of the expatriate population, the market impact of their presence is less by a substantial margin (notionally some 25 per cent) than their absolute incomes. Estimates of consumption in Kuwait for 1980 in the Family Budget Survey gave the following results:

Table 51   Household and per capita consumption by Kuwaiti and non-Kuwaiti communities — 1978/79 (KD)

Group	Consumption per month[a]	Consumption per year[a]	Consumption — total
Kuwaitis — by household	477.2	5,726.4	—
Kuwaitis — per capita	56.4	676.8	380,405,590
Non-Kuwaitis — by household	367.8	4,413.6	—
Non-Kuwaitis — per capita	56.6	690.0	539,123,150

Source: Family Budget Survey.
Note: a. less remittances abroad.

Total expenditures by the two sections of the population amounted to KD954,546,060 in 1980 of which the expatriate group accounted for 59.4 per cent. Private consumption in Kuwait is, however, only a relatively small part of total expenditures. The government sector, the combined government/private sector and the private sector acquisitions represent a far greater order of outgoings than private consumption. Central Bank figures showed private consumption as only 29.5 per cent of GDP in 1980. Import activities emphasise the comparatively lesser role of private consumption. In 1980 total imports were valued at KD1,7649 million. Of this, consumer goods, less re-exports, amounted to some KD488.8 million.[18] There was a continuing fall in the value of the consumer sector after 1980. The first three quarters of the year 1981 experienced a drop of this group of imports to 38 per cent of the total (*Quarterly Statistical Bulletin*, 1982, p. XII). It is evident that total government spending has been and is of growing significance in determining the volume of imports rather than the private sector consumer demand. Though this is not to deny that there is a linkage between the requirement for government expenditures and the size of the expatriate population and vice versa.

While a sizeable element of demand arises in each sector of the economy from the presence of the foreign population and is accounted for in the calculations offered earlier in this chapter, the most visible sign of the demand function of the foreign community is in the area of housing. Only Kuwaitis, with some few and unimportant exceptions, are permitted to own land and housing. A major economic interest of Kuwaiti businessmen has been development of quality housing for occupation by foreigners, since the latter have opportunity only for rent of their accommodation. A surplus of this standard of housing has been a feature of the market for some time. There were reported to be 180,400 occupied housing units in Kuwait in 1980, with 28,419 vacant and a further 5,629 under construction (Ministry of Planning, 1980 Census preliminary results, 1980, p. 20). A high rate of renewal of properties has characterized Kuwait over the last decade or so, but, none the less, it is clear that there has been a shortage of cheaper vacant property, causing an inflation of rents. Only high-priced apartments in locations distant from Kuwait City have been left vacant and there were numbers of modern blocks with occupation rates of less than 50 per cent in 1983. It might be deemed that the owners of these expensive blocks of apartments have an interest in ensuring that the foreign population is kept up so that they might reveal a profit on their investments. Meantime, though many individual Kuwaitis have investments in property for leasing to the expatriate community, the larger developments, made of extensive complexes of apartments, shops and other facilities, tend to be in the hands of commercial groups in which a small number of leading commercial families are involved.

Development and the domestic market

Much of the dilemma of the authorities in Kuwait in prosecuting management of oil income is a direct result of the nature of the State as an economy overwhelmingly dominated by oil. In 1981 oil exports accounted for 87.4 per cent of total exports, 100 per cent of government revenues, and 63 per cent of GDP. Stauffer has suggested that these figures, certainly in respect of GDP, understate the reliance on the oil sector of economic activities as a whole (Stauffer 1981). Kuwait appears by most criteria to be a *rentier* oil economy of the classic desert economy type (McLachlan 1980, p. 88).

In this position, which has become firmly established with the passage of time, the authorities have sought means of translating oil revenues into the domestic economy without creating disruptions such as severe inflation or taking direct roles in local expenditures to the exclusion of the private sector. Vehicles for transferring income through the private sector have proved less than perfect. Purchases of land from individuals was an early and continuing programme through which funds were moved into private Kuwaiti hands, though with considerable inefficiencies (IBRD 1965, p. 28). Since the 1950s, the Government has generally turned to other methods of fuelling the prosperity of the domestic market and has had notable successes in promoting development projects, often in conjunction with private companies.

Use of investment programmes within Kuwait as a means of stimulating the domestic market has effectively pumped funds into private sector activities and has had the social and political effect of satisfying, albeit less than fully, important Kuwaiti interests at a variety of levels not simply the major commercial families. The cost of such a policy has been to obscure the difference between priming the local market and initiating genuine economic development by way of creating permanent productive assets in the country. In this context, arguments become complex and diverge towards two principal ends. First, it is urged that real development has been foregone as a direct function of the State's need to appease the interests of the commercial groups. And further costs have been that the forms of State spending have caused, quite deliberately, the growth of the foreign labour force, since that has been part and parcel of the expansion of the economy in a way acceptable to Kuwaiti commercial interests. Second, there is a view keenly disliked by Arab observers that an oil-based economy such as that in Kuwait has few prospects of attaining viable non-oil development. This view is based on a variety of cogent reasons, including the difficulty in protecting infant industries, the lack of domestic resources other than hydrocarbons even down to fundamental factors of production such as fertile land and abundance of cheap water supplies,[19] the poverty of the indigenous labour force in skills, adaptability and motivation, and uncompetitive wage rates. Moreover, the strength of Kuwaiti oil reserves indicates that, under present world economic conditions, the country has little incentive to look for serious diversification of its economic structure for many years. In these circumstances, the authorities have few options than to find the least damaging means through which to transfer funds to the domestic market. Integral to such an approach has been expansion of the foreign community in Kuwait.

Assessment of the contributions to the Kuwaiti economy by the immigrant workers inevitably carries with it emotive overtones. Most views within Kuwait are emotionally inspired, whether from the indigenous or foreign side. Political attitudes, too, are never far from the surface during any debate on the issue of the foreign labour force. In this situation it is apparent that the question is clouded both by the lack of reliable information and by the confused balance of virtues and demerits of the foreign communities. The weighting of individual factors at play in the matter is often more a result of prejudice than considered judgement as social and economic variables are treated with equivalent importance. From the evaluation of the economic balances under review in this section of the study, it is apparent that the margins of costs and benefits are narrow or overlapping. Simplistic verdicts are not helpful and the authors refrain from making any in a situation where human and economic paradoxes abound.

Ultimately, perhaps, this study has tried to contribute to the debate by isolating where possible the variables that affect the balance between the utility and disutility of the foreign workforce. Appreciation on both sides of the mechanisms within the economic system that make the immigrant workers of all kinds vital to the functioning of the Kuwaiti system of handling the great difficulties of disbursing oil revenues in a way that sustains Kuwaitis in a prosperous if not always productive environment would be a major step forward. It is platitudinous but true that management of the oil-based economy has been effected largely by the introduction of the foreign workforce as a vehicle through which the local market has been kept more or less buoyant over a long period. This mechanism drew in foreign workers and has become reliant on them for its continuance to the present day. Since critics of the system have so far failed to elaborate a convincing alternative mode of economic progress for the State, it is likely to be maintained into the future. In this case, the foreign workforce appears to be a semi-permanent institution in Kuwait that must be accommodated to within an appropriate time frame. If Kuwait has regarded its immigrant population as a temporary phenomenon thus far, and this is the basis of most criticisms of the system among those that make up the expatriate groups, the authorities might draw the conclusion from this study that this is not sustainable and make suitable adjustments to attitudes and policies. For its part, the foreign community must appreciate the special circumstances that constrain Kuwaiti policies towards it.

Notes

1.   During the 1930s a number of Iranian families sought refuge in Kuwait from the modernizing policies of Riza Shah and there has been a continuing drift of people into Kuwait escaping from problems in their own countries that were only partially economic in nature. For the Iranian origin communities further reference can be sought in Razavian, M. T., *The Iranian Communities of the Persian Gulf*, Ph.D., London, 1975. The Arab communities of Palestine moved to Kuwait after 1948, though especially from 1963 following displacement from their homes during various bouts of the Arab-Israeli wars. Other examples of smaller-scale movements to Kuwait could be found by groups and individuals forcibly removed or harassed in their home territories. Whereas Kuwait has been generous in offering hospitality to those driven out elsewhere, it was not the only possible destination for those involved. A distinct choice was made in selecting Kuwait by most persons, including the Palestinians, and it may be assumed that estimates of financial and other welfare benefits were not least of their considerations.

2.   Interview with an employer of engineers, draughtsmen and other skilled grades of staff in April 1982 showed that he had lost two senior workers to Saudi Arabia and the UAE, respectively, in the previous six-months period. He felt that his position was symptomatic of the general situation in Kuwait at that time.

3.   Published information on the matter of wages paid to immigrant workers is extremely thin. In addition there are problems of comparability of incomes (and expenses) which make it difficult to do other than make a general assessment of a subjective nature, though this is precisely what mobile workers in the Gulf area must do for themselves.

4.   Of respondents to the 1981 survey, 16.4 per cent reported that their work in Kuwait imposed greater burdens than they could cope with. Only 31.5 per cent were engaged in occupations in which they had worked in their countries of origin.

5.   Results of the 1980 Census suggest in broad terms that significant numbers of the workforce were unregistered, possibly between 10 to 15 per cent of the total of those actively employed. Three main categories were involved: (1) illegal entrants smuggled into the state over land or sea borders, (2) persons who entered the state on visitor permits and who subsequently remained without permission, and (3) persons who entered on valid work permits but who stayed

after these had expired. The problems posed by the illegal workers have both economic and political dimensions for the Kuwaiti Government which defy easy solution.

6.   The problem of complementarity or parity between Kuwaiti and immigrant labour forces has never been seriously tackled. See in particular the observations and criticisms of Ismael Sirageldin, *Lecture on Population Policies and Development in the '80s*, Lectures in Development Economics No. 3, Pakistan Institute of Development Economics (undated), pp. 46-60.

7.   Population figures from National Censuses and GDP figures from Central Bank of Kuwait (at current prices).

8.   Assuming reserves at approximately 70,000 million barrels and output of 700,000 b/d.

9.   It was announced in March 1983 that the number of annual acceptances of foreigners for nationality would be lifted to a rate of 500. The permissions remained, however, mainly applicable to those Arabs residing in Kuwait before 1945 and other foreigners resident before 1930.

10.   The World Bank produced a *Core Planning Team Report on Long-term Development Strategy* in July 1981. Its findings were restricted but it has been reliably reported that IBRD forecast that the value of remittances from Kuwait would rise to KD537 million by the year 2000, p. 76.

11.   During the 1960s the annual average rate of growth was some 9 per cent. For the 1970s, the rate varied somewhat erratically though mainly above 10 per cent annually.

12.   The oil companies also brought in foreign labour to facilitate rapid expansion of the oil installations after 1951.

13.   Dr S. M. Al-Sabah has been a notable contributor to the study of women in the Kuwaiti economy and reference is invited to her book, *Development Planning in an Oil Economy and the Role of the Woman: The Case of Kuwait*, London, 1983.

14.   Interview at the Central Bank of Kuwait, March 1983.

15.   It is hoped that the imperfections of this calculation will prompt more sophisticated work by others solely concerned with national accounting.

16.   The Government of Jordan at one time argued strongly that it should be compensated by the States of the Gulf for its investment in education and training for the large Jordanian/Palestinian immigrant community working in the Gulf area.

17.   The Sample Survey of 1981 returned a figure of 59 per cent for those who took up their first job in Kuwait (Table 50).

18.   Total consumer goods imports were valued at KD756.5 million, while re-exports in SITC sections 1, 6, 7, and 8 were worth KD267.7 million.

19.   Professor Charles Issawi put forward the opinion that the poor resource base is of small consideration in any assessment of factors inhibiting Arab economic development. See Issawi, C., 'Why Japan?', in Ibrahim, I. (ed.), *Arab Resources: The Transformation of a Society*, London, 1983, pp. 283-300.

References

Al-Abdul Razzak, F. H., *Marine Resources of Kuwait: Their Role in the Development of Non-oil Resources*, unpublished Ph.D thesis, London University, 1979.
Alessa, S. Y., *The Manpower Problem in Kuwait*, London, 1981, pp. 2 and 111.
Birks, J. S., and Sinclair, C. A., *Arab Manpower*, London, Croom Helm, 1980, p. 36.

Birks, J. S., and Sinclair, C. A., *International Migration and Development in the Arab Region*, ILO, Geneva, 1980, p. 103.

Central Bank of Kuwait, *Quarterly Statistical Bulletins*.

Central Bank of Kuwait, *Quarterly Statistical Bulletin*, Oct.-Dec. 1982, p. XII.

El Mallakh, R., *Kuwait: Trade and Investment*, Boulder, 1979.

El Mallakh, R., *The Absorptive Capacity of Kuwait*, Lexington, 1981.

Fergany, N., 'Manpower projections in the Gulf', paper presented at symposium on Oil revenues and their Impact on development in the Gulf, Exeter (UK), 1982.

IBRD, *The Economic Development of Kuwait*, Baltimore, 1965, pp. 26 and 28.

McLachlan, K. S., 'Natural resources and development in the Gulf States', in Niblock, Tim, *Social and Economic Development in the Arab Gulf*, London, 1980, p. 88.

Middle East Economic Digest, 18.2.1983, p. 62.

Ministry of Planning, April 1982, *Bachelors Housing Study*.

Ministry of Planning, 1980, *Preliminary Results of the 1980 Census of Population, Housing and Establishment*, p. 20.

Seccombe, I. J., *Manpower and Migration: The Effects of International Labour Migration on Agricultural Development in the East Jordan Valley, 1973-1980*, Occasional Papers Series No. 11, Centre for Middle Eastern and Islamic Studies, University of Durham, 1981, p. 8.

Stauffer, T. R., 'Measuring oil addiction', *Middle East Economic Survey*, Vol. XXIV, No. 47, 1981, and 'Oil revenues: income or capital', MEES, 27.4.1983.

World Development Report, 1983, World Bank, p. 149.

5 THE RELATIVE STATUS OF IMMIGRANT WORKERS

5.1 Status of immigrant workers

Discussion in previous sections has made it amply clear that strains exist between the foreign labour force and their Kuwaiti hosts. While there are degrees of satisfaction for the immigrant group, by any measure they appear to be less well placed than their Kuwaiti co-inhabitants. It has been demonstrated by Alessa (Alessa 1981, pp. 44-50) that there is discrimination against foreign workers at all levels within Kuwait. While all of the conclusions reached by Alessa need not be accepted, his findings are adequately disturbing to demand more detailed attention.

Disadvantaging of the foreign workforce arises from the legal system within the State. Entry permits are granted only against the signature of a Kuwaiti guarantor, either private or institutional. Even where non-Kuwaitis act as equals within a legal entity such as a company incorporated in Kuwait, they are unable to act as guarantors for the entry of foreign workers on their own account. Residence in Kuwait and the accompanying permission to work depend on each foreign worker retaining the support of his guarantor and there is, in consequence, considerable personal and economic dependence by the immigrant on his Kuwaiti sponsor. In mitigation, it should be added that many Kuwaiti guarantors act within a traditional system of favours awarded on a quid pro quo basis and take little interest of an exploitative kind after the entry to Kuwait of a foreign worker for whom they are officially responsible. Indeed, he may have absolutely nothing to do with the worker once he has arrived in the country. For the unscrupulous, however, the guarantor system allows forms of exploitation of the foreign worker. One explanation of the high rate of mismatch between jobs in the country of immigrants' origin and that undertaken in Kuwait is that qualified persons applying for jobs in Kuwait find on arrival that their work is far below their qualifications and expectations. Wage rates tend to be similarly low and inappropriate to the job actually to be done. In such circumstances the immigrant may either remain in difficult conditions or return home, probably at his own expense.[1]

Kuwait has adhered, since independence, to creation of exclusive areas of activity for its own citizens. Non-Kuwaitis are disbarred from holding ownership of companies, real estate or other permanent assets unless in partnership with Kuwaitis, who must own 51 per cent or more of the equity. There are areas of the economy, too, that are excluded from activities by foreign interests. These include banking, financial houses and oil, among others. Discrimination in petroleum against American companies led in 1982 and 1983 to counter-measures against an affiliate of Kuwait Oil Corporation in the USA,[2] indicating the strength of negative reaction by one independent authority to the situation.

The *Kafeel* system, which demands Kuwaiti participation in companies as a prerequisite for foreign activities, has resulted in a large number of useful business arrangements that allow joint ventures to flourish to the benefit of both the domestic and foreign interests. It has also been a form of impediment on growth of the economy in so far as the foreign sector has been inhibited from independent action and all innovation has needed prior authorization by Kuwaitis, some of whom have been rather less qualified professionally than their foreign partners. The full impact of the enterprise of the foreigner group has been lost through the dampening effects of the *Kafeel* arrangement. At the same time, the system has given Kuwaitis a ready source of income and some have used their positions as sinecures or a reason for minimal participation in the economy, hence giving a double negative influence.

In the long term, exclusion of foreign direct involvement in the economy will achieve protection of the domestic interest. Continuing high levels of oil income could vindicate the policy, given, as argued earlier, that the companies taking part in development are simply being used as vehicles for moving resources into the domestic economy. If, on the other hand, Kuwait has recourse to diversification of its sources of income to supplement or substitute for oil revenues, the *Kafeel* system could prove extremely expensive. Overseas activities of Kuwaiti companies could be blocked in retaliation for constraints on foreign groups inside Kuwait. Development in Kuwait of financial services as a foreign exchange earning sector would equally be subject to considerable limitations. Unlike Bahrain, Kuwait notably failed to develop a role in provision of international financial services after the eclipse of Beirut as the Middle East regional centre, not least as a consequence of the inability of foreign banks to gain entry to Kuwait.

Comparative wages for the Kuwaiti and non-Kuwaiti sectors of the workforce

The legal and structural differences between the two sections of the workforce noted above tend, understandably, to have reflections in the wages earned. The position for the accompanied families included within the Sample Survey of 1981 was shown in Tables 37 to 42 showing appreciable differences between employees depending on factors such as educational status, age, occupation and location of residence.

Table 52   Average salaries paid by the Government, 1976 (KD/month)

Occupational category	Kuwaitis average	Non-Kuwaitis average
Technical professions	239	206
Other professions	251	190
Managers	556	503
Executive and clerical	198	158
Sales, etc.	162	80
Agriculture and fisheries	191	69
Production workers	220	106
Labourers semi-skilled	202	63
Unskilled labourers	189	67
Total — all groups	204	123

Source: *Annual Statistical Abstract*, 1981, pp. 136-40.

For the workforce as a whole, taking account of the single male workers, the situation is somewhat different. Up-to-date information is poor since the Family Budget Survey of 1978/79 did not disclose total incomes. Figures for 1976 are less than satisfactory, but they indicate the then differentials between Kuwaitis and non-Kuwaitis in salary terms. At that time, the average salary paid by the government to its Kuwaiti employees was KD204 per month against KD123 for non-Kuwaitis. In almost every sector of employment with the government the average pay of Kuwaitis was higher than the foreign workers in that area (Table 52). In most sectors, Kuwaiti pay was very much higher. Much of this difference is accounted for by the special allowances paid by the government to its indigenous workers and by the slightly senior position of Kuwaitis within the hierarchy of state organizations. None the less, excessive differentials of income in similar employment categories between Kuwaitis and the foreign workforce and between comparatively more skilled foreign workers in one grade against unskilled Kuwaitis in lower grades does little to encourage the overseas group to believe that their position is satisfactory. The data in Table 52 indicate that many unskilled Kuwaiti labourers earn as much as professionally qualified staff in the non-Kuwaiti workforce. Differentials of this kind have led in the past to Kuwait being described as a 'wage-slavery' economy.[3] Even if this is less than just, the position does little to enhance young Kuwaitis' perceptions of the role played by the foreign workforce and debilitates their own motivation to increase their overall role or their individual productivity. It is important, too, that the Kuwaiti foreign workforce contains a relatively large proportion of long-term residents, mostly Palestinian/Jordanians whose condition of life is scarcely any different from that of their Kuwaiti counterparts. As a result, while all differentials will tend to generate forms of resentment, short-term workers have opportunity to accept the situation or to withdraw their labour. Longer-term residents are not in so favoured a position given the real constraints upon them and have cause to feel deeper though repressed dissatisfaction (Al-Moosa 1983).

Existence of wage differentials is a function of the balance of fear among the foreign workforce that individuals can be deported almost at will,[4] that employers can exert undue influence simply by implementing the law of guarantor against his employees if they threaten resignation, and that there is no organization to protect their interests. Development of trade unions in Kuwait is best described as cosmetic. Kuwaitis have associations that overtly stand to defend labour. Foreign workers are not permitted to group together in trade unions. In the market place in Kuwait they find themselves in a totally vulnerable position, therefore, though the inefficiencies of the bureaucracy and the general laxity of employers tend to alleviate the worst aspects of the situation.

Satisfaction expressed by respondents during field survey in Kuwait in 1981 in respect of their lives in the country was considerable (Table 53). But it cannot be totally accepted that such satisfaction is entirely positive. Each of the foreign communities has special reasons for its presence in Kuwait, many of which give little choice to many individuals in their selection of and continuing stay in the country. In this situation, wage rates and issues such as ownership of property are less important than the *force majeure* that operates for so many of the expatriate community. Such considerations are underlined by the fact that 45 per cent of respondents were Palestinian/Jordanian by origin. The Egyptians, too, tend to be a special case as will be demonstrated in the next section of this chapter.

Table 53   Expressed satisfaction with life in Kuwait, 1981 – Foreign Labour (%)

	Satisfied	More or less satisfied	Dissatisfied
Female	68.3	27.8	3.9
Male	71.8	24.1	4.1
Total	68.9	27.2	3.9

Source: Sample Survey of 1981.

Housing and the immigrant worker

Among the vexed questions that arise among the foreign population is that of property ownership in Kuwait. As described previously in Section 3.4, non-Kuwaitis, whatever their status or length of residence, are unable to own the title of any real estate. The high rents charged for accommodation and the poor quality of the housing available for rent make the situation worse.

The location of such housing partially disguises a second form of discrimination against foreign residents. There have grown up sections of the urban area that are in fact exclusively occupied by Kuwaitis and those that are predominantly occupied by non-Kuwaitis. The causes of this are partly administrative. Some districts are developed by the government solely for low-income Kuwaitis. Similarly, housing areas in which plots are granted for house building are only for Kuwaitis. Elsewhere, especially for those in well-paid occupations whether Kuwaiti or non-Kuwaiti, high-class housing in apartments or villas is available and inter-mixing of the communities is normal. There are other housing areas, mainly in zones abandoned by Kuwaitis or that have been redeveloped, where lower-paid foreign workers live but it is claimed with justice that these areas given over predominantly to the expatriate community are less well served than the main Kuwait housing districts.

Stability of the workforce

The stability of the foreign workforce in Kuwait is affected by two main variables. First, there is the peculiarity of the Palestinian/Jordanian section of the total who are not entirely mobile. Second, there are considerations of the desirability of Kuwait for other workers who have real alternatives to working in Kuwait. They each form very different parts of the foreign community by attitude and more objective criteria such as structure and involvement by economic group.

It is estimated that there are approximately 250,000 persons of

Palestinian origin in the State on the basis of the Census of 1980. They form no less than 23 per cent of the total population and more than a quarter of all Arabs resident in Kuwait. The Palestinian community is of long-standing. There has been an erratic growth in its numbers, especially in the period after 1948, when refugees came with each reverse in the war against Israel. The wars of 1956, 1967 and 1973 all brought further exoduses of Palestinians to Kuwait, while there was a further lesser movement following the invasion of Lebanon in 1982 by the Israeli army and the scattering of the Palestinian refugee communities in that country. Meanwhile there was a rapid growth in Palestinian numbers inside Kuwait as a result of natural rates of increase that more than competed with the endemically high indigenous growth rates.

In addition to the numerical importance of the Palestinians as a community, they also form a large and important part of the workforce. It is estimated that they represent some 40 per cent of the total in 1980 according to the latest official estimates. Perhaps their most significant feature, however, is their comparative permanency. While the Palestinians do not have official rights to permanent residence in Kuwait and few have been granted Kuwaiti nationality on a permanent basis (374 persons were reported at the 1975 Census as having Kuwaiti nationality but born in Jordan and Palestine)[5] there is a tacit arrangement whereby the Palestinian community lives in Kuwait without molestation. From the workforce point of view this has meant that the presence of the group has given a considerable stability to the foreign workforce as a whole that would otherwise have been less marked.

The range of Palestinian labour inputs into Kuwait is widespread. They form very significant fractions of each of the main categories of the workforce (Table 22). They have a very special role in the State as providers of artisan inputs in such areas as mechanical and electrical engineering and the semi-skilled occupations within the construction industry. It is a truism, also, that they comprise a docile part of the workforce. With few exceptions they have participated in the development of Kuwait without demanding special consideration. Even as members of the community at large they are among the most law-abiding.[6] Of all the sections of the foreign workforce they might have been expected to demand fairer treatment in areas such as wages and conditions of work, since they are long-term residents with the same living problems as are faced by the Kuwaitis themselves. At the same time they had experience of organized labour under the British Mandate in Palestine and are aware of the benefits that accrue to labour from associations of working people.

The explanation of the quiescence of the Palestinian community is complex in general but rests on a single simple factor. Unlike other foreign workers, the Palestinians have a very limited choice of alternative places to which they can migrate for residence and work. Political, social and economic discrimination against them in many parts of the world arising from their lack of nationality status for purposes of their travel documents has precluded all but a favoured élite from moving to the industrialized states, though there are now sizeable communities of Palestinians in the USA and Canada. Their position in the Arab world is little better. They are officially welcomed everywhere in the Middle East except Israel but, in reality, few Arab governments offer equality of conditions to the Palestinians either as citizens or members of the workforce as to their own nationals. For all the problems in Kuwait experienced by the Palestinians, they are better off there than in almost every other country of the Arab world.

In consequence, the Palestinians have been careful to retain their positions in Kuwait by taking a socially and economically low profile. For the Kuwaitis, the effects have been to give a maturity to the workforce by way of experience that would otherwise be missing and to give a stability to the core of the labour force by length of stay as shown in Table 1.

Other groups have exhibited very differing characteristics. A number of other special relationships exist, including one with Iran, which has been the case for many years (Razavian Ph.D. thesis, unpublished, 1976). Iranians, often from specific areas in Iran sometimes defined at the village level, have been migrating to Kuwait on a semi-permanent or seasonal basis to service requirements in construction, marine activities and the special needs of the Iranian-origin population of Kuwaiti nationality. While it is true that a proportion of Iranian labour migration to Kuwait has been illegal, especially of seasonal labour from Khuzestan, Kermanshahan and other areas of the western Iranian provinces, there has also been legal and semi-permanent transfer to Kuwait. Although, therefore, entirely separate from the Palestinians, parts of the Iranian community have functioned as a reinforcing factor in stabilizing the foreign workforce. Only in their tendency to come as single unaccompanied workers do the Iranians differentiate themselves from the Palestinians as factors in giving a strong element of continuity to the labour force.

For other nationalities the trends are less clear. Stays are shorter for those in the labouring group. But there are fairly large numbers of

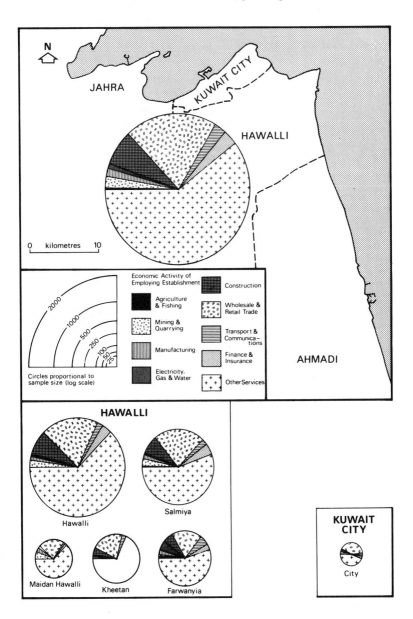

Figure 5.1   Percentage distribution of immigrant workers with previous jobs in Kuwait by district

professional and senior technical grades that remain for extended periods in Kuwait. Egyptians in particular are within this category (see Section 3.6). In other areas of the labour force, however, there is a deep instability. Stays tend to be short on the average and from time to time Kuwait has been less competitive for labour than other states in the Gulf region, partly on grounds of lower wages paid and partly since general conditions of service have been better elsewhere. The emergence of the Gulf Cooperation Council which intends to equalize conditions throughout the region, might take some of the pressure off this area of differentials for Kuwait. The world recession, too, has had the same impact, with foreign labour generally less able to move at will as a result of falling levels of economic activity throughout the Gulf region as well as in their countries of origin since 1980.

Productivity of the labour force

Note has already been made of the poor skill levels brought in by migrants and the tendency of the Kuwaiti market to use foreign labour in a general purpose way. Assessment of the productivity of the foreign workforce has not been undertaken in depth. Available data indicate that productivity levels are low. The total value of output of the expatriate working community was put at KD1,361.5 million in 1980, providing 56.9 per cent of GDP. On a per capita basis this averages KD3,577 per year. Real unit productivity is less easily arrived at in relation to levels achieved elsewhere in comparable countries. Observation shows that there is in Kuwait a visible element of 'disguised unemployment' in so far as an appreciable number of foreign workers are engaged in marginal activities such as newspaper selling and minor services of the same type. The productivity of such occupations must be low by any measure, which makes little economic sense in an economy such as that in Kuwait. It is also the case that Kuwaitis use a large proportion of their foreign labourers as household servants. It is estimated that the current ratio of Kuwaiti families to servants is 1:2.2, which gives an aggregate of more than 150,000 in this category assuming that all Kuwaiti households have servants.[7]

There must be doubt concerning those foreign workers who come to Kuwait to take up their first jobs or who fill posts in Kuwait for which they have no previous training. Productivity for them must for the most part be poor or less than that standard expected in a profit-motivated economy.

The undertaking of menial tasks by foreigners in Kuwaiti homes and in general services does not appear to release Kuwaitis for more demanding occupations. Despite the extensive use of foreigners in households as housemaids, drivers and child minders, the Kuwaiti rate of participation in the labour force at large remains extremely low (males 32.2 per cent, females 4.8 per cent and the average 19.1 per cent). In effect, foreign labour is used in menial tasks to substitute for Kuwait inputs, which are then consumed in leisure activities.

A further aspect of productivity that has received little attention has been the depressing influence of a large and often ill-trained foreign workforce in Kuwait on the adoption of labour-saving technologies. Systems of construction, one of the largest consumers of labour in the country, are often labour-intensive using primitive wooden scaffolding, manual setting of concrete frames and walling, and laborious means of putting floors or secondary fixings in place. Low-budget housing areas are particularly notable for their labour-intensive approach to building. Road construction, administration of the civil service and other aspects of the economy show similar features that appear to be at odds with the real needs of a small-population country that incurs heavy financial and social costs for its import of foreign labour. It might be argued that easy access to cheap, albeit under-qualified, labour has deterred the country from looking for more appropriate capital-intensive methods for expanding its economy and making it more efficient. With the passage of time, the State has become tied into the cheap labour syndrome and now operates and plans its forward activities on the basis of the availability of cheap imported labour. Yet the real interests of Kuwait might be better served through improving internal efficiency, first by mechanising activities to enable rising Kuwaiti productivity per indigenous inhabitant and, second, by mobilizing rather more thoroughly than at present the Kuwaitis for participation in economic activities by making access to foreign labour more difficult or more expensive. Such a move would automatically tend also to force up levels of productivity among the expatriate workforce itself.

Planning of the economy has never made much progress in Kuwait. Its impact on real events has been even smaller. Lack of planning has certainly prevented formulation of long-term approaches to use of the labour force and productivity factors within it. Strategies for better use of Kuwaitis in economic occupations and for improving the contribution of the foreign labour force might be more likely to emerge within the framework of a medium-term plan than from a single year current and investment account budgets with a short-time horizon. Given the inter-relationship between the issue of labour force requirements, the role of the foreign population of the State, the composition of the

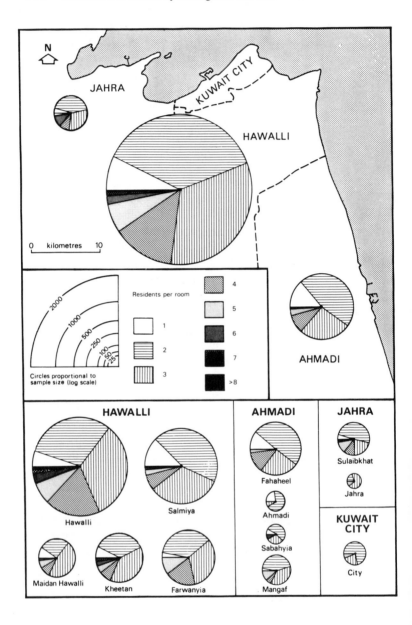

Figure 5.2   Percentage distribution of immigrant workers by economic activity of employing establishment and by district

Kuwaiti community and the question of nationality, it might be that planning has been avoided in order to obviate the need for a clear strategy on these issues. Costs of uncertainty, at least as expressed in productivity terms, have, however, been high.

The foreign labour force as employers and employees

The Census of 1980 produced data on commercial establishments in Kuwait indicating the distribution of employers and employees by Kuwaiti and non-Kuwaiti origin. The results of the survey suggest surprisingly high numbers of foreign residents as employers. Of a total number of 26,748 employers, 19,635 were non-Kuwaiti (Table 54). There were only between five to six persons per establishment for the group as a whole, indicating the small scale of businesses in Kuwait. Since foreigners are disbarred from setting up companies or other trading entities in Kuwait, those foreigners classified as employers will either be partners in formal businesses with Kuwaiti counterparts or run small and informal establishments on their own account.

Table 54   Distribution of establishments by regions, 1980

| Governorate | Number of establishments | | Employers | | Employees | |
	Private	Government	Kuwaiti	Non-Kuwaiti	Kuwaiti	Non-Kuwaiti
Capital	17,637	660	4,247	7,863	2,364	101,478
Hawalli	13,535	686	1,994	8,620	627	54,335
Ahmadi	4,005	455	286	2,171	3,500	32,146
Jahra	2,531	272	586	981	376	11,586
Total	37,708	2,073	7,113	19,635	6,867	199,545

Source: Preliminary Results of the Census of Establishments, Ministry of Planning, 1980, p. 27.

The comparative standing of the Kuwaiti and foreign workforces is clear from Table 54, with the former accounting for only 3.3 per cent of the total employees and 26.6 per cent of the employers. The dominating role of the Capital Governorate, with more than half of all persons engaged in commercial establishments is shown, together with the comparatively tiny contribution of Jahra, where total population numbers are low and development in the sense of economic activities have come recently. Ahmadi has its position supported by both the existence there of a large number of oil-related establishments (the ratio of private to government establishments was 10:1 against much lower ratios elsewhere) and by recent growth of housing areas within its borders, which has brought commercial development in its wake.

Table 55   The ten major districts of location of establishments, 1980

Rank	District	Total establishments	Total employed
1	Qibla (Capital)	8,766	41,388
2	Shuwaikh Industry (Capital)	2,558	34,927
3	Sharq (Capital)	2,092	12,911
4	Ray (Hawalli)	1,058	12,536
5	Shuaiba and south coastal strip (Ahmadi)	130	12,344
6	Ahmadi City (Ahmadi)	432	10,786
7	Hawalli (Hawalli)	3,230	10,704
8	Sulaibikhat (Capital)	2,228	10,547
9	Salmiya (Hawalli)	2,549	10,384
10	Murgab (Capital)	1,200	7,774

Source: Preliminary Results of the Census of Establishments, Ministry of Planning, 1980, pp. 28-31.

Within Kuwait there is a very high degree of differentiation between residential and commercial areas. Commercial establishments tend, therefore, to be extremely concentrated into designated zones, especially marked in the Capital Governorate, where half of all persons engaged in this sector are concentrated (Table 55). Together, the top ten areas account for more than 70 per cent of all those reported as employed in establishments. The geographical concentration is even more remarkable when the districts are isolated to show those of the above list that are adjacent. Kuwait City, for example, takes in Qibla, Sharq and Murgab as a central business district, with Ray and Shuwaikh slightly to the west of it. Salmiya and Hawalli form another grouping, while Ahmadi City, Shuaiba and Sulaibikhat make separate discrete blocks isolated from the main residential areas, the former two concerned principally with the oil industry.

The proportion of foreigners in the labour force is high in those areas where industry is concentrated and where small-scale commercial enterprise is most in evidence. Kuwaitis, accounting for 5.7 per cent of the total number employed in all establishments in the survey, were poorly represented almost everywhere. Only in Qibla, where they were slightly less than 10 per cent of the total employed, was there a significant presence of Kuwaitis.

Table 56   Geographical distribution of Kuwaiti and non-Kuwaiti
            populations —   1980

Kuwaiti majority	*Mixed areas*[1]	*Non-Kuwaiti areas*[2]
Capital Governorate		
Dasma	Dasman	Sharq
Mansouriya		Morgab
Daiya		Salhiyah
Abdulla Salem		Qibla
Shamiyah		
Qadisiya		
Nuzha		
Fayha		
Keifan		
Hawalli Governorate		
Sha'ab	Jabriya	Hawalli
Rawda	Salwa	Salmiya
Adeliyah	Surra	Maidan Hawalli
Khaldiyah	Qurtuba	Messila
Rumaithiya	Yarmouk	Farwaniya
Omeriyah	Abrak Kheitan	Ray
Rabiya	Jaleeb al Shuyukh	Reqai
Saihed al Awazem	Ardia	New Kheetan
Mushrif	Bayan	
Ain Baghzi		
Ahmadi Governorate		
Reqa	Funtas	Provisional dwellings
Sabahyia	Abu Halifa	
Umm al Himan	Mangaf	Mina Saud[4]
Ahmadi City	Wafra[3]	Fenitees
Desert Area		Mahbula
Aghailah		
Jahra Governorate		
Sulaibikhat		
Doha		
Scrap Area		
Jahra Area		
Asheesh al Jahra		
Desert Area		
Sulaibiyah		

1. Mixed areas include those where Kuwaitis form not less than one-quarter of
    the total according to the data of the 1980 Census.
2. Non-Kuwaiti areas comprise those where Kuwaitis form less than a quarter
    of the total community recorded in the 1980 Census.
3. Wafra has an agricultural scheme, workers for which are foreign.
4. Mina Saud is in the divided Neutral Zone and is populated mainly with Saudi
    Arabian bedouin people.

5.2   An assessment of the costs of immigrant workers to the Kuwaiti economy

Costs of the foreign workforce to Kuwait can be seen only against the benefits they bring. Any other form of assessment would of necessity be misleading and mischievous. This review will set out to examine the several apparent costs of the presence of the expatriate workforce in Kuwait. However, it must be kept in mind that the existence of the foreign workforce and the total foreign community is not entirely in parallel. A very substantial portion of the non-Kuwaiti population is made up of persons of Palestinian origin whose position in the country is that of political refugees first and foremost. It is only a consequence of their arrival in Kuwait following a political decision to accept the Palestinians as refugees that they became members of the workforce. They would be present even if not part of the legitimate labour force. At the same time, both Palestinian and other elements of the foreign community form a valuable asset for the Kuwaiti economy and this discussion acknowledges that position, though mainly concerned with the burden of costs that is required to maintain them in the State.

Of a total of 1,355,827 persons registered in the Census of 1980 there were 793,762 non-Kuwaitis. Some 40 per cent of the foreign community was made up of Palestinians (including those with Jordanian passports). Since these people are political refugees and would be in Kuwait regardless of the labour force requirement, it is moot whether their costs should be attributed to the foreign labour force at all. Possibly a more logical approach to the Palestinians would be that they are defraying Kuwait's costs for its own political decisions by contributing to the Kuwaiti national income. Such a logic would not be attractive to most Kuwaitis since the political decision to take in the Palestinians was made many years ago before Kuwait became legally independent. The policy of offering sanctuary to the Palestinians has not been officially renounced and Kuwait continues to maintain the *status quo* in this area although many Kuwaitis would wish to treat the Palestinians from the economic point of view in exactly the same way as all other members of the expatriate workforce. In this brief survey it will be assumed that the Palestinians must be taken on the same basis as the other foreigners and that costs incurred by them are to be attributed to the economic rather than the political domain.

Economic costs

The Kuwaiti exchequer incurs a range of costs on account of the foreign community within the State. Calculation of the precise *incremental* costs of servicing the foreign population has problems of both methodology and implementation. And however appropriate the methodology, the data base is inadequate to bear detailed scrutiny needed to determine with accuracy the capital and current costs called for solely to maintain the expatriates. Yet, with the foreign group making up almost 60 per cent of the total population in Kuwait in 1980, it is clear that there are heavy overhead costs to bear disproportionate to the small Kuwaiti base. The situation is exacerbated by the welfare state that operates, which serves both indigenous and foreign populations in most areas, thereby generating rather more expenses on account of foreigners than would be the case in most other countries.

Despite Kuwaiti generosity, there is not parity in access to services. The point has already been made that Kuwaitis live in better areas as defined by availability of services, type of housing, standard of environment and use of domestic labour. In education, university entrance strongly favours Kuwaitis. Job opportunities, job security and conditions of employment are all funded through state coffers for the benefit of Kuwaitis. The comparative privilege of access to services by Kuwaitis defies any simple universal formula for attributing costs of the social services and infrastructure on a group-by-group basis used, for example, in the calculations in Section 4.4. Recent studies of income per inhabitant, offering figures for both the Kuwaiti and non-Kuwaiti groups (Table 51), suggest that there is virtual parity of consumption (Family Budget Survey 1980, Ministry of Planning). This may be so[8] but it would not necessarily indicate that there was also parity of total consumption of goods and services, including those provided by the government on a cost-free allocation.[9]

In order to compensate for the higher level of goods and services available to Kuwaitis and often their better quality, an entirely subjective assumption has been made after talks with various authorities both Kuwaiti and non-Kuwaiti that a factor of two shall be used to multiply Kuwaiti shares of services and other benefits against that allotted to the foreign group. On this comparatively simple basis the costs of the foreign workforce as assessed by the current costs incurred by the government appear as follows:

Table 56   Costs to Kuwait of the foreign workforce, 1981/82
(KD/mn)

Defence, security and justice	124.8
Education	89.6
Health	64.0
Information	12.9
Social and labour affairs	17.8
Electricity and water	113.5
Public works	19.7
Communications	12.3
Customs and ports	4.1
Finance	13.0
Oil	1.1
Planning	7.8
Housing and government properties	0.4
Amiri court	52.4
Unclassified and transfer expenditures	319.1
Land acquisition	126.9
Investment expenditure	
Public works	75.1
Electricity and water	123.9
Communications	5.2
other	2.9
Total	1,186.5

Source: Central Bank of Kuwait, *Quarterly Statistical Bulletin*, Oct.-Dec. 1982,
p. 19.
Note: Non-Kuwaiti share calculated 1:2 against the Kuwaitis by size of
population = 42.3 per cent attributable to the foreign community.

It might be suggested on the basis of a 1:2 ratio between costs for Kuwaitis against non-Kuwaitis calculated on population sizes in 1980, that approximately 40 per cent of current and investment costs can be allocated to the foreign section of the community. Some KD1,186.5 million were expended in these areas by the government in the financial year 1981/82 from a total budget of KD2,805.5 million. If the land acquisition programme expenses[10] in Table 56 are omitted as being entirely inapplicable to the non-Kuwaitis in the population, the total relevant costs drop to KD1,059.6 million, or 37.8 per cent of all outgoings in the annual budget.

The foreign labour force carries some opportunity costs for Kuwait. Two of these have already been mentioned, including the under-development of the Kuwaiti labour force as a result of the substitution of foreigners in a number of sectors of activity. The extremely low participation rate of Kuwaitis is only possible because foreigners undertake jobs that would otherwise be forced upon Kuwaitis. This has to be assumed to be negative from the point of view of the long-term elaboration of a mature indigenous structure of the labour force. Additionally, the reality of the semi-permanent foreign group demands that policies for the application of high technology and capital-intensive means of development and administration are foregone to the detriment of improved productivity by the Kuwaiti workforce.

On a more material level, the employment of foreigners is consumption of income, a large portion of it foreign exchange resources. It could be argued with some merit that each foreigner employed is equivalent to the abstention from investment in alternative assets. On a crude basis, the costs of the foreign labour force diminish on a more or less *pro rata* scale the funds that could otherwise have been available for placement overseas in portfolio investments earning a steady income. Plainly, not all foreign workers could be done without. But, given the existence of disguised unemployment and the substitution of foreigners for Kuwaitis (as reflected in participation rates), there must be a significant proportion of the foreign workforce for which there is an opportunity cost of the kind described.

Social elements

There have been visible social costs arising from the presence in this small state of large numbers of foreigners. It is a perception general among Kuwaitis that they have been socially and culturally swamped by the arrival of large numbers of foreigners. While it might be indicated in mitigation that more than four out of every ten members of the non-Kuwaiti community are Palestinians and there by Kuwaiti invitation as part of the State's contribution to the Arab cause in Palestine, such considerations find few positive responses in many nationals. Meanwhile, the movements of foreign labour to Kuwait have principally concerned people of Arab origin. In addition to the Palestinians, there is a further 20 per cent of the total population made up of Arabs to give the total non-Kuwaiti Arab population of more than 40 per cent of the entire community and an Arab population overall of approximately 90 per cent. For all the Arab cultural nature of the foreign workforce and its accompanying community, the Kuwaitis have felt no less socially constrained. Their minority status within their own country has become more of a social problem as the populations of the non-Kuwaiti Arabs have grown and in some ways Kuwaitis appear to feel more assailed by the Arab elements in the foreign workforce than by those from entirely different foreign societies such as Europe, USA and the Far East.

Symptomatic of the siege mentality of the Kuwaitis has been their grouping into areas quite separate from the foreign elements wherever possible. The strongly defensive attitude of Kuwaitis is also illustrated by the low level of grant of nationality status to foreigners (Table 57). Indeed, the debate on the matter of nationality has ceased to be a live issue despite some remaining pressures.[11] There are few Kuwaitis to be found who would welcome the grant of nationality *en masse* to expatriates nor even for those persons born in Kuwait and in fact permanently resident in the State (amounting to approximately 100,000 persons in 1980). By the early 1980s the combination of insecurities had been reinforced by a deteriorating financial situation arising from declining oil revenues and falling levels of overseas earning from investments. Taken together with forecasts of poor prospects for the international oil market and the debilitating effects of financial grants to neighbouring Iraq to assist it during its economic difficulties caused by the war with Iran, it appeared to many educated Kuwaitis that there was need for economic retrenchment. This included protecting the indigenous population from further call on the State's finances by naturalization of large numbers of aliens. In effect, the oil and financial resources of the country were to be conserved for the existing population to the exclusion of others. At heart, however, economic problems served mainly to legitimize emotional sensitivities on the question of Kuwaiti nationality for parts of the foreign workforce.

Table 57   Naturalization, 1971-1979

1971	1972	1973	1974	1975	1976	1977	1978	1979
4,662	5,509	7,201	8,148	7,388	8,930	6,661	7,514	8,760

Source: *Annual Statistical Abstract*, 1981, p. 51.

Evaluation of the effects of the foreign community on the social structure of Kuwait has been undertaken (Al-Naqeeb, *Journal of Social Sciences*, January 1978, pp. 271-236). Before the influx of foreigners on a large scale, Kuwaiti society was conventionally divided into groups comprising, respectively, the ruling family, the merchants and the rest. Relationships within this system were complex and rarely entirely stable (Al-Munais, unpublished Ph.D. thesis 1981). Introduction of the oil economy brought rapidly rising individual incomes for most Kuwaitis and also the presence of the foreign workforce. Differentiation between the Kuwaitis and the foreign community, with the former retaining the bulk of the financial and social privileges, had diverse effects. In relative terms, the Kuwaitis were forced increasingly into taking on attitudes and functions that might elsewhere be deemed to be 'middle class'. On income grounds, certainly, a large number of Kuwaitis were to be seen as well off. Many engaged in trade, ownership of property for profit, investment in Kuwait and purchase of assets abroad. Either at the commercial or the domestic level, Kuwaitis became employers of (foreign) labour. This trend was not universal, since there were poorer Kuwaitis who were government employees and who either did not see or could not afford opportunities to develop ownership of factors of production. The only claim to capitalist activity among such people was ownership of their houses through assistance from the government, though this was often enough to give them an adequate vested interest in property.

Once the foreign labour is taken into account, the relative status of the Kuwaitis is enhanced. What might have appeared within a purely Kuwaiti framework as a socially modest position, becomes one of privilege when set against the expatriate. Expressed in access to educational, employment and housing, the privileges of the native Kuwaitis in areas from which the non-Kuwaitis are excluded produce a special class which in many ways defies conventional analysis but which could be deemed to make by far the majority of Kuwaitis effectively 'middle class' in the sense that they are superior socially inside their country to all foreigners but not the equal of their own ruling group (Fergany Exeter 1982, p. 8). The overt symbol of Kuwaiti social differentiation from the non-Kuwaitis is the wearing of national dress on most public occasions.

In addition to the general placing of the mass of Kuwaitis in an intermediate social position between the foreigners below and the political élite above, there has been the growth of a middle class with characteristics more akin to those normally accepted as middle class within Western terms of social analysis. The trading families in particular have for the most part consolidated their role as risk-takers and capitalists. The group has been augmented considerably by the accession to it of numerous small traders on their own account, property developers, dealers in foreign exchange and owners of sufficient capital to be of independent financial means. It is not known with certainty how many Kuwaitis maintain bank accounts abroad, but portfolios of foreign investments held by the private sector earned an estimated KD337.7 million in 1979, implying that not inconsiderable numbers of Kuwaitis acted in a capitalist capacity abroad even if not in Kuwait itself.

In so far as education has fed the process of development of the

Kuwaiti social élite, its role is, on paper at least, significant. Enrolments at Kuwait University have risen steadily and with them the number of graduates (Table 58). A further spurt to the definition of the intellectual élite has come through taking advanced academic or applied study abroad.[12] While the size of the educated middle class remains modest, it is a group with growing influence and status.

Table 58   Enrolments and graduations in Kuwait University, 1975-1979

Kuwaitis	1975/76	1976/77	1977/78	1978/79	1979/80
Enrolments	2,801	3,977	5,452	5,721	6,682
Graduations	400	432	503	645	899

Source: *Annual Statistical Abstract*, 1981, pp. 371-3.
Notes: a. Enrolments for 1980/81 were 6,544.
　　　　b. Enrolments from 1977/78 for First Semester only.

The bedouin in Kuwait pose a severe problem for conventional classifications. Those that have Kuwaiti nationality are in receipt of housing from the government, while all bedouin have the right to work regardless of nationality status. Many are employed by the government as guards, policemen and in the army, though there were many who took part in small-scale commercial activities such as driving light vans and other occupations. The Kuwaiti bedouins without nationality are not in receipt of housing of right and have an intermediary status of being accepted but not integrated, though Kuwait has made growing efforts to solve the related problems of the bedouin and their housing situation.[13] Officially, they form part of the foreign community but in reality act as if they were full nationals and fulfil the role of a non-manual working class in the same way as those bedouin with nationality.

In summary, it might be said with some truth that the presence of a large non-Kuwaiti workforce, the majority involved in manual labouring and production tasks, has made all Kuwaitis into one form of privileged élite or another. All those predilections of the Kuwaitis not to be engaged in manual work[14] have been enhanced. Whether the virtual embourgeoisement of Kuwaitis and their general opening up to travel and to exposure to international influences of a cultural kind are to be regarded as costs attributable to the foreign workforce is a moot point. That the presence of the foreign workforce was responsible for so rapid and complete a transfer of the population to a class that might objectively be considered as an intermediate or even 'middle class' has to be accepted.

Notes

1.   The example is drawn with acknowledgement from the research among agricultural labourers in the Wafra area of Kuwait by Dr S. Mutawa of the University of Kuwait. Verbal communication, March 1983.

2.   Santa Fe Company, majority owned by Kuwaiti interests, was banned from award of licences for operations in national territories in the USA as a tit-for-tat for exclusion of US interests from similar work in Kuwait.

3.   Stories of the effects of the differential abound in Kuwait. Alessa quotes the case of a newspaper report in which a Kuwaiti watchman who was entirely illiterate earned more than three times the monthly salary of the foreign school teacher engaged at the same government establishment. Alessa 1981, p. 44.

4.   Some 9,651 persons were deported in 1980. There were claims that as many as 50,000 persons were deported in 1982 under an amnesty for foreigners contravening residence regulations.

5.   Officially, policy of Arab governments towards the Palestinians has been not to give nationality on the grounds that they will ultimately return to their homeland.

6.   In 1980 Palestinians made up a mere 1.1 per cent of those committing reported crimes in the country despite the fact that they are the largest single foreign group in the State.

7.   There were reported to be 69,523 private Kuwaiti households in 1980. The number of persons actually registered in this employment group in the same year was reported at 56,170, or 12 per cent of non-oil employment or one in every seven non-Kuwaitis in employment. In reality, the number is probably higher since part-time domestic service and the registering of persons under other categories is common.

8.   The authors of this volume have reservations concerning the enumeration of the Family Budget Survey. The nature of the sampling appears to have brought a strong bias against higher income group Kuwaitis. The latter were excluded, apparently on the grounds that one or two extremely large incomes of the millionaire class would distort the findings of the survey. Private communication, March 1983.

9.   In housing, the government provides land, housing loans and/or housing to Kuwaitis by right. The foreign community does not benefit in this way by either income or capital appreciation.

10.   The State has carried on a programme of land acquisition from Kuwaiti nationals since the 1950s as a means of stimulating the local market and transferring oil income to individual Kuwaitis. It has no direct meaning for the non-Kuwaiti group.

11.   Alessa, 1981, devotes time to the question and presses the case for the naturalization of long-term Arab residents (Palestinian presumably).

12.   There were 175 Kuwaitis studying for postgraduate degrees in foreign universities in the year 1980/81 with a further 2,558 engaged in undergraduate courses or equivalent training abroad in the same year.

13.   The problems of the bedouins in the shanty (Asheesh) areas of Kuwait are looked at in detail in Al-Moosa, A. A., *Bedouin Shanty Settlements in Kuwait; A Study in Social Geography*, unpublished Ph.D. thesis, London University, 1977.

14.   Assuming that such a tendency is not universal.

15.   Middle class being defined here as property-owning, capitalist or employer of persons or subsister off unearned income. The pejoratives of the Marxists are not intended nor seen as relevant. Note, too, that since all Kuwaitis live in a *rentier* economy based on oil, they might be deemed to be capitalists by definition.

References

Alessa, S. Y., *The Manpower Problem in Kuwait*, London, 1981, pp. 44-50.

Al-Moosa, A. A., *The Degree of Satisfaction of the Foreign Labour Force in Kuwait*, 1983.

Al-Munais, W. A. A., *Social and Ethnic Differentiation in Kuwait: A Social Geography of an Indigenous Society*, unpublished Ph.D. thesis, London University, 1981.

Al-Naqeeb, K. H., 'Social strata formation and social change in Kuwait', *Journal of Social Sciences*, Kuwait, Vol. 4, January 1978, pp. 271-236.

Family Budget Survey, 1980, Ministry of Planning.

Fergany, N., 'Manpower problems and projections in the Gulf', paper delivered at the Symposium on Oil Revenues and their Impact on Development in the Gulf States, Exeter, 1982, p. 8.

Razavian, M. T., *The Iranian Communities of the Persian Gulf*, unpublished Ph.D. thesis, London University, 1976.

6 CONCLUSIONS AND FUTURE OUTLOOK

6.1 The political dimension of the immigrant workforce

There has been a deep reluctance in Kuwait to face up to the challenges of the presence of a large and difficult-to-manage workforce. It has been shown already that government policies have been short-term and inconsistent in treatment of the immigrants who make up so large a section of both the labour force and the population at large. Realistic calculation of the economic costs and benefits of the presence of so many foreign workers has not yet been attempted. Not surprisingly, the political dimension of the perceived threat from the immigrants is even less explicitly assessed. In consequence, the subject has become invested with suspicion and prejudice to the extent that trust between the Kuwaiti and non-Kuwaiti communities has been severely eroded. Certainly, there is apprehension concerning the government's desire to banish the foreign community regardless of its utility value to the economy and the claims of individual groups, especially of Arabs, to privileged hospitality. In private and by innuendo, the immigrants in Kuwait can be left with few doubts that their futures in the State can be anything but certain.

Among the results of the growth of the foreign workforce in Kuwait has been the bringing into play of a range of domestic and foreign pressures of a political kind. At home, the Kuwaitis are vastly outnumbered and have continually to assert their positions as effective rulers, employers and managers of their economy. There is a perception among Kuwaitis that aspects of Kuwait commercial policy are affected by the presence of communities with external relations inside the country. This is particularly the case with the larger groups of Arabs, including the Palestinians and the Egyptians. The presence of the Palestinians can never be entirely divorced from the activities of the Palestine Liberation Organization and the general Arab cause on the Palestine issue. In principle, Palestinians are treated on the same basis as all other foreigners. Even where a Palestinian was born, educated and had all his family in Kuwait, he would have no more right than any other nationality to re-enter Kuwait after having left for anything other than a holiday. Yet the fact remains, that the Palestinian community has been large and stable as measured by population size, despite very considerable feelings of fear and antipathy towards it by some Kuwaitis. Continuing existence of the Palestinians in Kuwait as one in five of the total population suggest that there has been no systematic attempt to reduce its size by the government and that, as argued earlier, the economic role of the Palestinians as part of the foreign workforce comes in the wake of, or parallel to, political considerations.

Action to diminish the numbers of other elements of the non-Kuwaiti national groups has similar constraints. Events have shown that the authorities have been cautious to move against disruptive parts of its foreign community in order not to upset its relations with other states. The Egyptians in Kuwait comprise less of an immediate political problem,[1] though even here there have been perceptible limits to government responses to them even when they have clearly been in contravention of Kuwaiti law.[2] In 1982 large numbers of foreign labourers were given the opportunity to leave Kuwait under an amnesty for those contravening residence and labour laws. It is thought that, of those who took advantage of the amnesty,[3] as many as half returned to Kuwait through legal channels in its immediate aftermath.[4] While the Kuwaiti economy was clearly buoyant enough to absorb most of this labour and created the demand for them, the authorities were not willing to alienate the major Arab states beyond a certain point.

From the results of this study it is apparent that government policies towards the foreign workforce on the political level have constraints. The origin of these constraining influences is never entirely obvious. Kuwait has always been circumspect in its relations with its powerful neighbours in all aspects of its policies. It has a difficult position as a small undefendable but rich state in a region of considerable political volatility. At the same time, it has an integral role within the mainstream of Arab politics from which it cannot divorce itself. Internally, it cannot afford the alienation of the largest section of the population which is foreign even if mainly Arab in origin. There are internal pressures, too, within Kuwaiti circles for the special treatment of particular sections of the foreign community, where, for example, prominent Kuwaitis act as sponsors for a nationality group working in Kuwait and defend their interests by working inside the domestic political system.[5]

The total effect of such influences is to limit freedom of action by the authorities in respect of the foreign labour force to token punishments and expulsions while leaving the essential fabric of the foreign communities almost untouched. Ultimately, the government appears to have used exclusion of groups from initial entry as a tool of control rather than acting against it once it has become installed inside the country. Some entrants to Kuwait have found it difficult to break in through the official channels in recent years.[6]

6.2 Conclusions

The costs of the foreign workforce to Kuwait can be seen to be varied but often incalculable. Arguments on appropriate methodologies for analysing the outgoings on account of the foreign community as a whole are interesting but not entirely relevant in a country where the statistical base is improving but inadequate for finely tuned evaluation of specific variables. It would seem that the overhead costs of the presence of the foreign community at large are significant, amounting possibly to approximately 40 per cent of the Kuwaiti annual budget. At the same time, there are undoubted negative factors by way of the opportunity costs to Kuwait of the foreign workforce. Social and political prices have to be paid for the maintenance of a majority group of non-Kuwaitis, which are constant irritants to the indigenous population. It is feasible to argue, too, that the foreign community has inadvertently but quite perceptibly pushed Kuwaiti society to becoming structured in a way different from any normal economic community, with its members clustered in the intermediate and the ruling classes and almost completely absent from the manual occupations, the landless groups and those excluded from manipulation of the factors of production. The latter are taken up by non-Kuwaitis. Even in its external relations, Kuwait has to take some cognizance of the position of the foreign communities and has limits to its freedom of action in a number of areas because of this.

Costs of the foreign workforce and the non-Kuwaiti community in general are offset by the positive factors of their contribution noted in Chapter 4. In fact, the large foreign group remains because its role is indispensable to the Kuwaitis. The expatriate workers of all kinds made it possible for the State to be developed rapidly from the 1950s. Neither the welfare programmes, on which the country began development during the 1950s and 1960s, nor the expansion of the physical infrastructure of housing, roads, ports and other facilities could have been implemented without the use of large numbers of foreign workers. Manual, semi-skilled, artisan, management and technological inputs were provided from outside since the domestic labour force was entirely inadequate by size or training to undertake the task.

Steady priming of the economy by government expenditure programmes has kept up the pace of construction and sustained an appreciable measure of prosperity in the domestic market, which has, in turn,
required underpinning by imported labour. Even the development of
the Kuwaiti educational system, the one route through which, eventually, there might be some substitution of immigrants by indigenous
people, has been undertaken by means of foreign teachers and administrators.

In the final analysis, two features stand out in balancing the costs
and benefits of the foreign community and deserve recapitulation here.
First, the foreign workforce would not remain in Kuwait unless either it
was gainfully employed or it had no other place where it could find
refuge. The very laws in Kuwait governing foreign labour ensure that
those leaving employment must quit the country within two weeks of
the expiry of their jobs. While it is true that there is a measure of viola-
tion of this law by various means, including over-staying the period of
residence and entering Kuwait illegally in the first place, the law is
operative in by far the majority of cases sooner or later. Until recent
years, immigrants had opportunity to move from Kuwait if they felt
that better opportunities existed for employment elsewhere. Iranian
and Iraqi labour moved back to its country of provenance during the
economic booms in those countries during the early to mid-1970s,
indicating that mobility did exist. In the late 1970s and early 1980s, it
was reported that numbers of other labourers transferred from Kuwait
to other oil-exporting states of the Gulf area in response to higher wage
rates operating there. There is evidence, therefore, that there is real
demand in Kuwait for labour that can only be supplied from outside
the State. This is not to deny, however, that there is an element of the
foreign workforce in Kuwait which is better off there under-employed
and comparatively low-paid than in its country of origin because of
the enormous differential that exists between living standards in Kuwait
and those prevailing elsewhere.

Second, the basic problems of the authorities in Kuwait in managing
an oil-based economy has remained more or less unchanged by principle
even if altering by scale since oil came to be the main support of the
country some thirty or more years ago. There is a need to transfer oil
income into domestic prosperity, which can be effected in a limited
number of ways. The chosen way for Kuwait has been a high degree of
pump priming of private sector activities through government spending.
The means used for this end have been land purchases, grants of housing, and inception of 'development' projects in both the commercial

and infrastructural sectors of the economy. Parallel to this policy has been the generation of welfare benefits for Kuwaitis and guaranteed employment in the civil service. Both lines have been reinforcing of each other. The sum effect of this system of management has been that foreign staff have been sucked into the domestic economy to enable projects to be constructed and run within the framework of the pump priming mechanism. Provision of state employment for Kuwaitis has *de facto* created the need for others to undertake manual tasks elsewhere in the economy, to sustain the private sector at all levels of employment and to provide skilled inputs where Kuwaiti resources were inadequate. The foreign community, comparatively well paid and in one case in two accompanied by members of the family, became an important part of the domestic market. Demand in some forms was embarrassing, as in the case of housing, but, in general, the foreign community was a strong element of demand for goods which had the economic and political virtue of feeding prosperity among the merchant houses and retail traders in Kuwait.

The costs and benefits of the presence of the foreign workforce defy easy quantification. Yet the balance between the two sections of the society as evaluated in economic terms is by no means one-sided. The foreign workforce has become economically vital to Kuwait in providing a range of services and skills beyond the scope of the indigenous community in both spread of activities and numbers required. There would be an inevitable and rapid decline in the wealth of the State following the withdrawal of the foreign groups. The domestic level of production would fall and consumption, too, would be affected on a serious scale.[7] Buoyancy would entirely vanish from the domestic trading sector. Judging by the high proportion of foreign labour in some sectors, there could be entire areas of activity that would vanish if non-Kuwaitis withdrew.

In a structural sense, the appreciable diminution of the foreign community would result in a severe skewing of the society. In practice, Kuwait would lose its working class and large numbers from the ranks of the educated élite and from the skilled artisan group. Perhaps in time Kuwaiti society itself could adjust to the new situation, though it would take a long period in which to do so and a radical alteration of traditional attitudes to enable Kuwaitis to take up manual occupations in substantial numbers.

6.3   Considerations for the future

In the long-running debate concerning the foreign workforce in Kuwait the assumption is often made that the foreign workers are dispensable. From the results of this study it would seem that such a basis for argument is unhelpful. Objective criteria demonstrate that the question at issue is not whether or not the State requires a workforce drawn from abroad, for evidence shows that a workforce is needed from external sources and, although this requirement might fluctuate, it will be essential for many years.

Given that levels of demand for goods and services in Kuwait require fulfilling with the assistance of foreign labour, the only real point of contention is its composition. Kuwait does have some options to influence the sources, the marital status, the length of stay and the qualifications of its foreign workers. There would seem to be a strong case for the Kuwaiti authorities to demand better from its foreign workforce than in the past. Certainly, there is a need for more proven skills to be deployed. The Kuwaitis must also be educated in their use of the foreign workforce. Large resources are given over to the employment of unskilled general labourers for domestic purposes in Kuwaiti households, for which there is rarely economic justification, though medical and social reasons might vindicate a small portion of the total employment on this score. Even in business, there is widespread exploitation by Kuwaitis of all-purpose labour without proper training and opportunity for use in a productive fashion. But even where changes in the composition of the labour force might be desirable and can be brought about in practice, this will take time to have an effect not least since such changes will only be feasible in parallel with significant alterations in official policies, private attitudes and the legal and administrative framework within which immigration takes place.

To an extent also, the emotional aspects of the debate on the foreign workforce are rather a set of reactions to the presence of the expatriate populations as a whole, often failing to take account of the fact that the cost to the Kuwaitis of the departure of the foreign communities is the loss of the majority of the workforce. Yet the burden of the economic analysis in this study has shown that the nature of the Kuwaiti economy has been determined by the oil-base on which it rests and the particular mode of translating foreign exchange into local use adopted since the rise to importance of the oil sector during the 1950s. It must be concluded, therefore, that to remove the foreign workforce (a vital component of the economic management in Kuwait to the present) will also need a change in economic strategy. So far, the opponents of the foreign labour force and its communities inside Kuwait have failed to offer a model for evolution that might function better than that which exists. Other oil-based economies seem to offer no easy alternatives to the one now extant in Kuwait since few have, on the whole, operated as efficiently and smoothly,[8] despite the criticisms levelled by economists (Sayigh 1978). Without attempting to be geographical determinists, the authors find themselves of the belief that the extremely limited natural resources of Kuwait, allied to the special problems of an oil-based economy rehearsed in this volume give scope for few other approaches to oil fund management than its disbursement into the domestic economy through what often appear to be pseudo developments in commerce, industry and infrastructure. It is reasonable for Kuwaitis at times to be irritated by some of the more crude forms of pseudo development and to be excited by the day-to-day problems of the presence of the foreigners in their midst as the majority group, but, without the offer of a realistic alternative, they would be advised to adhere to that which works rather than turn in exasperation to models that are untried or uncertain in outcome.

The role of the immigrant workers in sustaining the economy in its present form has produced increasing friction between Kuwaitis and their now unwelcome guests. It might be suggested that this study has shown that transference of guilt and blame to the foreign community for the State's intractable problems does little justice to the real situation. The basic and most important steps towards changing the balance of workforce and population in Kuwait to the benefit of the indigenous people are first, that they themselves become more dedicated to involvement in the harsh and dirty tasks of daily manual or technical work within the country; second, that more Kuwaitis, both male and female, are prepared to join the labour force by abandoning a leisured life or undertaking training in useful skills, and, third, that Kuwaitis forego the guarantee of state-provided sinecure employment. All these measures lie in the domain of the Kuwaitis. Their impact on the immigrant workforce would start slowly but ultimately become dramatic by way of reducing demand for foreign workers. Most of all, however, the change in attitudes implicit in the three elements noted above would bring a new ethos to Kuwaiti society as a whole that would lay the ground for more optimism for the economic future of the State than is presently justified, since it would have its roots in an *active* participation of Kuwaitis in the development and maintenance of their country.

It must be expected that a continuance of current government policies and private attitudes will not produce any significant changes in participation rates, availability of skills or heightened productivity by Kuwaitis. The best that might emerge from the contemporary debate on immigrant workers and the foreign community in Kuwait will be *passive* solutions. These will concern altering the rate and style of development so as to minimise demand for the non-Kuwaiti labour. More stringent controls on the entry and residence of foreigners were already being implemented by early 1984 as a further move of the same sort.[9] Budgetary allocations for construction and other sectors used by the government to transfer resources to the private sector were reduced in 1983 and 1984.

The findings of the research programme push the authors to take the view that *passive* solutions represent political appeasement and economic temporising. Real and lasting change will be signified only by the clear dedication of the Kuwaitis themselves to long-term self-reliance in labour supply, though, as a final caveat, it must be made clear that improvements would initially be slow and hard-won — leaving this option as the one least inviting from a political point of view and therefore the less likely to be taken up.

Notes

1.   Before 1970 it was generally assumed that Egyptians abroad had a surrogate political role as ambassadors of Arab nationalism.

2.   Violations of the law were generally in the form of over-staying residence permission or working without authorization.

3.   As many as 50,000 persons were thought to be involved in the expulsions.

4.   Some 15,000, mainly Egyptians, are estimated to have returned shortly after their departure. Private communication, March 1983.

5.   Specific sponsors have in the past used their positions in the upper echelons of the Kuwaiti political/economic systems to defend national groups, e.g. the Behbahani family for certain Iranians (Razavian, *The Iranian Communities of the Persian Gulf*).

6.   Iraqis as a proportion of those granted labour permits fell from 3.2 per cent in 1975 to 2.9 per cent in 1979 during which time total numbers of permits granted rose by 35.1 per cent.

7.   A number of shops in Kuwait reported a marked decline in their sales towards the end of 1982 and in early 1983 as the foreign workforce contracted as a result of expulsions and a deteriorating level of economic activity inside Kuwait. Daily takings were down from KD350 to KD100 per day in one particular case in Kuwait city centre.

8.   In 1983, for example, Kuwait was one of a tiny number of Arab states that were not suffering from the effects of the recession in world trade through severe debt exposure. While a deficit on the current budget was expected, this was well able to be handled through withdrawals from reserves. In that same year,

most OPEC states were in debt, in arrears on paying suppliers and were facing radical cut-backs in state spending.

9.   The under-secretary of the Ministry of the Interior was reported as announcing that the government was determined to end its policy of permitting the entry of foreign labour. He said that a committee had been formed to assess the necessity of each foreign employee to local companies. *Financial Times*, London, January 13, 1984, p. 3.

Reference

Sayigh, Y. A., *Economies of the Arab World*, 1978, pp. 81-126.

APPENDIX

Statistical tables supporting the text. (Data derived from fieldwork undertaken under the supervision of Dr A. A. Moosa in the period 1980-83.)

Table 1   Period of stay in Kuwait by nationality

| Nationality | Period of Residence | | | | | | | | | |
	Less than 5 years Total	%	5-9 years Total	%	10-14 years Total	%	More than 15 years Total	%	Total Total	%
Palestinians and Jordanians	26	3.4	72	9.5	116	15.3	546	71.8	760	100.0
Arabs from the Arabian Gulf	5	17.9	1	3.6	3	10.7	19	67.8	28	100.0
Egyptians	111	27.5	160	39.6	67	16.6	66	16.3	404	100.0
Other Arabs	41	13.4	36	11.8	41	13.4	188	61.4	306	100.0
Indians	23	27.4	22	26.2	18	21.4	21	25.0	84	100.0
Pakistanis	7	20.6	8	23.5	2	5.9	17	50.0	34	100.0
Other Asians	18	42.8	1	2.4	7	16.7	16	28.1	42	100.0
Other nationalities	21	77.8	4	14.8	–	–	2	7.4	27	100.0
Stateless persons	–	–	–	–	–	–	4	100.0	4	100.0
Grand Total	252	14.9	304	18.0	254	15.0	879	52.1	1689	100.0

Source: Sample Survey 1981.

Table 2   The foreign labour force by length of stay

Length of stay	1981 Sample Survey Number	%	1980 Census Number	%
Less than 5 years	252	14.9	358,688	45
5-9 years	304	18.0	178,724	23
10-14 years	254	15.0	126,694	16
15 years and over	879	52.1	128,233	16
Total	1689	100.0	792,339	100

Source: Sample Survey 1981 and *Annual Statistical Abstract*, 1982.

Table 3 Per cent labour force by nationality and highest qualifications

	Illiterate	Read and write	Primary school	Intermediate school	Secondary school or equivalent	University and above	Total
Kuwait	36.4	14.3	21.7	16.2	9.0	2.4	100.0
Non-Kuwaiti	24.2	22.1	16.0	14.2	14.7	8.8	100.0
Total	28.9	19.0	18.1	15.1	12.5	6.4	100.0

Source: *Annual Statistical Abstract*, 1982.

Table 4 Educational standard by occupation of the foreign labour force in Kuwait

	Scientific and technical	Administrative and managerial	Clerical	Sales	Service	Agriculture and fishermen	Production and labourers
Illiterate	–	–	1.3	2.7	58.7	1.3	36.0
Read and write	5.5	0.5	9.1	13.2	23.2	2.3	46.4
Below secondary	12.8	2.1	16.8	15.7	10.2	1.0	41.4
Below university	41.1	4.8	34.1	8.5	0.6	–	10.8
Graduates	80.2	6.8	10.2	1.8	0.7	–	0.4
Total	41.2	4.1	17.3	8.2	8.6	0.6	20.0

Source: Sample Survey 1981.

Table 5   Educational standard of the foreign labour force in their country of origin by occupation

	Scientific and technical	Administrative and managerial	Clerical	Sales	Service	Agriculture and fishermen	Production and labourers
Illiterate	–	–	4.6	4.6	22.8	38.7	29.5
Read and write	3.2	–	5.8	9.1	12.3	29.9	39.6
Below secondary	12.8	–	10.4	16.6	5.2	16.6	38.4
Below university	49.4	2.1	25.3	7.7	1.3	1.7	12.4
Graduates	79.2	8.8	8.5	2.3	0.8	–	0.5
Total	44.5	3.8	12.1	7.5	4.4	9.8	17.9

Source: Sample Survey 1981.

Table 6 Standard of education by length of stay in years

	Less than 5	5-9	10-14	15 and more
Illiterate	20.0	8.0	8.0	64.0
Read and write	7.7	6.8	11.7	73.9
Below secondary	6.3	10.2	12.1	71.4
Below university	11.6	17.5	17.1	53.8
Graduates	25.2	29.2	17.7	27.8
Total	14.9	18.0	15.0	52.0

Source: Sample Survey 1981.

Table 7 The foreign labour force by age group

Age Group	Male	Female	Total	%
15-19	15,812	2,347	18,159	4.7
20-24	45,679	6,962	52,641	13.7
25-29	65,984	16,673	76,657	20.0
30-34	62,255	9,460	71,715	18.7
35-39	50,433	7,115	57,548	15.0
40-44	40,780	5,653	46,433	12.1
45-49	25,717	3,361	29,078	7.6
50-54	16,040	2,036	18,076	4.7
55-59	7,308	885	8,193	2.1
60 and over	4,672	617	5,289	1.4
Total	334,680	49,109	383,789	100.0

Source: *Annual Statistical Abstract*, 1982 (Table 84).

Table 8 Foreign labour force: sex by age group

	Less than 30	30-	40-	50 and over	Total
Male	14.7	33.9	34.8	16.6	82.8
Female	38.6	41.0	16.0	3.8	17.2
Total	18.8	35.1	31.7	14.4	100.0

Source: Sample Survey 1981.

Table 9   Age group by occupation in Kuwait

Age / Occupation	Scientific and technical	Administrative and managerial	Clerical	Sales	Service	Agriculture and fishermen	Production and labourers
Less than 30	33.2	1.9	23.3	9.9	13.4	–	18.2
30-	48.7	4.6	17.4	6.6	6.4	0.3	16.0
40-	44.0	3.6	16.1	7.1	8.1	0.7	20.4
50 and over	26.9	7.0	12.0	12.4	9.1	1.7	31.0
Total	41.2	4.1	17.3	8.2	8.6	0.6	20.0

Source: Sample Survey 1981.

Table 10   Age group by feeling of settlement in Kuwait

	Perfectly settled	*Somewhat settled*	*Not settled*	*Age group as percentage of total*
Less than 30	69.7	23.3	6.9	18.8
30-	66.5	29.3	4.2	35.1
40-	69.7	27.7	2.6	31.7
50 and over	72.0	25.9	2.1	14.4
Total	68.9	27.2	3.9	100.0

Source: Sample Survey 1981.

Table 11   Age group by intention of stay

Age Group	Years	Do not know	Less than 3	3-	5-	7-	9-	11-	15-	17-	21 and over
Less than 30		85.0	4.7	3.0	2.7	0.3	1.0	—	0.3	—	3.0
30-		79.4	6.8	5.1	2.8	—	1.0	—	—	—	4.9
40-		83.4	3.3	4.4	3.5	—	0.6	0.4	0.4	0.2	3.9
50 and over		83.2	5.5	3.4	2.5	—	0.8	—	—	—	4.6
Total		82.3	5.1	4.2	2.9	0.1	0.9	0.1	0.2	0.1	4.2

Source: Sample Survey 1981.

Table 12   Age group by nationality

	Palestinians and Jordanians	Arabs from the Arabian Gulf	Egyptians	Other Arabs	Indians	Pakistanis	Other Asians	Others	Stateless
Less than 30	39.0	1.6	19.5	24.8	5.3	3.1	4.4	1.6	1.0
30-	42.9	2.7	29.0	14.1	4.9	2.2	1.7	2.2	0.3
40-	46.5	1.1	25.4	16.6	4.9	1.7	2.4	1.3	—
50 and more	54.7	0.4	14.0	22.2	4.9	0.8	2.1	0.8	—
Total	45.0	1.7	23.9	18.1	5.0	2.0	2.5	1.6	0.2

Source: Sample Survey 1981.

Table 13   Sex by marital status

	Single	Married accompanied by spouse	Married unaccompanied	Divorced	Widow/widower
Male	8.6	88.1	3.1	0.1	0.1
Female	19.0	70.0	3.4	2.8	4.8
Total	10.4	85.0	3.1	0.5	0.9

Source: Sample Survey 1981.

Table 14   Sex by educational standard

	Illiterate	Read and write	Below secondary	Below university	Graduates	Total
Male	3.4	14.3	25.1	24.1	33.0	82.8
Female	9.3	7.6	10.3	34.8	37.9	17.2
Total	4.4	13.1	22.6	26.0	33.8	100.0

Source: Sample Survey 1981.

Table 15   Sex by occupation

	Scientific and technical	Administrative and managerial	Clerical	Sales	Service	Agriculture and fishermen	Production and labourers	%
Male	38.1	4.8	16.5	9.8	6.2	0.7	23.9	100
Female	56.4	0.7	21.3	0.3	20.6	—	0.7	100
Total	41.2	4.1	17.3	8.2	8.6	0.6	20.0	100

Source: Sample Survey 1981.

Table 16   Sex by length of stay in Kuwait

	Less than 5	5-9	10-14	15 and over
Male	12.1	16.7	14.6	56.6
Female	28.6	24.1	17.2	30.0
Total	14.9	18.0	15.0	52.0

Source: Sample Survey 1981.

Table 17   Sex by length of intention to stay, in years

	Do not know	Less than 3	3-	5-	7-	9-	11-	15-	17-	21 and over
Male	83.7	4.3	3.5	2.9	0.1	1.0	0.1	0.2	0.1	4.0
Female	75.0	8.8	7.7	2.9	—	0.4	—	—	—	5.1
Total	82.3	5.1	4.2	2.9	0.1	0.9	0.1	0.2	0.1	4.2

Source: Sample Survey 1981.

Table 18   The labour force: Kuwaitis and immigrants by selected occupations in 1957 and 1980

	1957		1980		Rate of increase		1980 Ratio
	K	non-K	K	non-K	K	non-K	K: non-K
Agriculture and fishing	603	446	3,938	5,212	553	1,070	1:1
Mining and quarrying	1,211	4,194	2,397	4,262	98	1.6	1:2
Manufacturing and industries	1,029	5,582	3,179	38,081	208	582	1:12
Construction	378	8,025	1,206	95,893	219	1,094	1:80
Wholesale and retail trade	4,151	4,073	4,577	53,840	10	1,222	1:12
Transportation and communication	1,513	2,053	7,832	22,321	418	987	1:3
Service	14,681	29,219	75,461	144,992	414	396	1:2
Others	4,807	3,590	4,884	15,969	1.6	345	1:3
Total	28,373	57,182	103,474	380,570	265	566	

Source: 1957 and 1980 (sample) Census.

Table 19   Foreign labour force by selected occupations

	1957		1980	
	Total	*%*	*Total*	*%*
Production labourers	38,440	67.2	169,885	44.6
Professional and technical workers	3,299	5.8	62,286	16.4
Service workers	5,180	9.0	77,065	20.3

Source: 1957 and 1980 Census.

Table 20   Kuwait — percentage distribution of the non-Kuwaiti workforce by employment category, 1975, 1980 and 1981

	Total non-Kuwaiti workforce		*Non-Kuwaiti workforce accompanied by family*
	1975	*1980*	*Sample survey of 1981*
Professional and scientific	15.2	16.4	46.5
Administrative and managerial	0.8	1.0	4.9
Executive and clerical	9.5	9.3	12.9
Sales	8.5	6.8	7.0
Services	21.5	20.3	6.0
Agriculture and fishermen	1.8	1.6	0.9
Production and labourers	42.7	44.6	21.8
Total	100.0	100.0	100.0

Source: Sample Survey of 1981 and National Censuses.

Table 21 The foreign labour force by nationality and their occupation in their home countries

	Professional and technical	Administrative and managerial	Clerical	Sales	Agriculture and fishermen	Production and labourers	Services
Palestinians and Jordanians	32.7	1.2	9.2	8.2	19.9	22.3	6.5
Arabs from the Arabian Gulf	9.1	–	36.3	27.3	9.1	18.2	–
Egyptians	66.6	6.4	14.1	3.1	0.9	4.9	4.0
Other Arabs	33.8	3.6	10.2	14.5	8.4	25.9	3.6
Indians	38.7	7.5	26.9	3.1	1.5	20.9	1.5
Pakistanis	33.3	–	4.8	9.5	–	52.4	–
Other Asians	13.6	4.5	9.1	13.6	13.6	45.6	–
Others	84.0	8.0	4.0	4.0	–	–	–
Total	44.4	4.2	12.1	7.4	9.8	17.8	4.3

Source: Sample Survey 1981.

Table 22 The foreign labour force by nationality and their occupations in Kuwait

	Professional and technical	Administrative and managerial	Clerical	Sales	Agriculture and fishermen	Production and labourers	Services
Palestinians and Jordanians	35.8	4.4	19.0	7.5	1.3	25.1	7.0
Arabs from the Arabian Gulf	28.6	7.1	25.0	16.7	–	25.0	3.6
Egyptians	68.3	2.0	14.9	2.5	6.0	5.2	7.2
Other Arabs	23.8	5.6	15.2	17.9	–	24.8	12.6
Indians	33.3	4.8	29.8	8.3	–	14.3	9.5
Pakistanis	24.2	6.1	15.2	9.1	–	45.5	–
Other Asians	19.0	–	4.8	7.1	–	35.1	33.3
Others	81.5	7.4	3.7	3.7	–	3.7	–
Total	46.5	4.9	12.9	7.0	0.9	21.8	6.0

Source: Sample Survey 1981.

Table 23 The geographical distribution of the total population and labour force in economic establishments in the four Governorates (1980)

| | Population | | Employees | |
	Kuwaitis	Immigrants	Kuwaitis	Immigrants
Capital	12.7	13.9	34.4	51.1
Hawalli	36.4	68.7	9.1	26.9
Ahmadi	24.1	12.2	50.9	16.2
Jahra	26.7	5.2	5.5	5.8
Total	100.0	100.0	100.0	100.0

Source: 1980 Census.

Table 24   Geographical distribution of selected nationalities in main areas in 1975

	Egyptians			Palestin. and Jordan.*			Other Arabs**			Iranians			Indians			Pakistanis		
	% Immg.	% Total pop.	%	% Immg.	% Total pop.	%	% Immg.	% Total pop.	%	% Immg.	% Total pop.	%	% Immg.	% Total pop.	%	% Immg.	% Total pop.	%
Kuwait																		
Town	19.6	16.6	21.5	8.9	7.5	2.9	15.2	13.0	9.1	16.2	13.7	26.3	19.0	16.1	39.3	9.0	7.6	26.0
Salmiya	15.8	13.3	25.4	43.7	37.3	20.8	19.7	16.8	17.2	5.5	4.7	13.0	4.5	3.8	13.7	3.5	3.0	15.0
Hawalli	9.5	8.7	18.9	60.0	55.5	35.5	20.4	18.9	22.2	2.7	2.5	8.0	1.7	1.6	6.4	1.5	1.3	7.7
Maidan																		
Hawalli	17.7	16.4	6.0	45.9	42.2	4.6	22.5	20.7	4.1	4.8	4.4	2.4	3.4	3.1	2.2	0.8	0.7	0.7
Kheetan	3.8	2.2	2.2	54.9	32.7	9.5	18.5	11.0	5.9	4.6	2.4	4.0	1.0	6.6	0.9	4.0	2.4	6.1
Farwaniya	3.4	2.7	2.0	74.0	58.3	12.8	7.9	9.2	2.5	1.9	1.5	1.6	0.5	0.4	0.5	7.3	5.7	11.2
Fahaheel	6.5	4.0	2.3	45.1	28.3	4.6	14.6	9.1	2.8	8.0	5.0	4.1	8.0	5.0	5.2	9.1	5.7	8.3

Source: 1975 Census, Volume 3, Table 47.
*Palestinians and Jordanians. **Iraqis, Syrians and Lebanese.

Table 25 Distribution of immigrant workers by nationality and district

	Palestinians and Jordanians %		Gulf Arabs %		Egyptians %		Other Arabs %		Indians %		Pakistanis %		Others %		Total %	
Hawalli	53.6	309	2.1	12	19.4	112	21.1	122	1.2	7	0.7	4	1.9	11	100.0	577
Salmiya	37.8	134	1.4	5	30.2	107	21.2	75	2.0	7	0.6	2	6.8	24	100.0	354
Maidan Hawalli	35.6	31	–	–	28.7	25	31.0	27	2.3	2	–	–	2.4	2	100.0	87
Kheetan	36.6	51	2.2	3	29.5	41	9.4	13	7.9	11	8.6	12	5.8	8	100.0	139
Farwaniya	53.2	99	1.6	3	31.2	58	7.5	14	3.8	7	1.1	2	1.6	3	100.0	186
Total Hawalli Governorate	46.5	624	1.7	23	25.5	343	18.7	251	2.5	34	1.5	20	3.6	48	100.0	1343
Kuwait City	–	–	–	–	20.0	5	8.0	2	72.0	18	–	–	.		100.0	25
Al-Ahmadi																
Fahaheel	39.3	64	1.8	3	7.4	12	18.4	30	17.2	28	6.1	10	9.8	16	100.0	163
Al-Ahmadi	23.9	5	–	–	19.0	4	–	–	19.0	4	19.0	4	19.1	4	100.0	21
Sabahyia	38.6	10	3.8	1	26.9	7	11.5	3	–	–	–	–	19.2	5	100.0	26
Mangaf	68.2	30	–	–	18.2	8	13.6	6	–	–	–	–	–	–	100.0	44
Total Al-Ahmadi Governorate	42.9	109	1.6	4	12.2	31	15.4	39	12.6	32	5.5	14	9.8	25	100.0	254
Al-Jahra																
Sulaibikhat	39.3	22	1.8	1	39.3	22	19.6	11	–	–	–	–	.	:	100.0	56
Jahra	50.0	6	–	–	25.0	3	25.0	3	–	–	–	–	–	–	100.0	12
Total Jahra Governorate	41.2	28	1.5	1	36.7	25	20.6	14	–	–	–	–	–	–	100.0	68
Total		761		28		404		306		84		34		73		

Source: Sample Survey 1981.

Table 27   Source of housing rent payment by percentage

Nationality	Employer	Self
Palestinians and Jordanians	4.5	95.5
Arabs from the Arabian Gulf	8.0	92.0
Egyptians	21.7	78.3
Other Arabs	9.4	90.6
Indians	7.7	92.3
Pakistanis	24.0	76.0
Other Asians	13.6	86.4
Others	71.4	28.6
Total	10.7	89.3

Source: Sample Survey 1981.

Table 28   Monthly housing rent paid by the foreign labour force (KD)

	Less than 30	30-	50-	70-	90-	110-	150-	190-	230-	Average
Palestinians and Jordanians	1.4	24.4	30.9	17.4	8.8	9.1	5.1	1.9	1.0	78.2
Arabs from the Arabian Gulf	13.1	13.1	8.7	8.7	17.4	4.3	30.4		4.3	105.0
Egyptians	1.5	4.6	23.9	21.4	13.3	23.0	8.2	3.6	0.5	99.4
Other Arabs	1.0	15.6	25.8	19.0	11.2	12.7	9.8	2.0	2.9	92.9
Indians	—	2.1	12.5	12.5	12.5	22.9	29.1	6.3	2.1	128.5
Pakistanis	15.8	10.5	26.3	15.8	—	15.8	10.5	5.3	—	85.3
Other Asians	5.3	10.5	15.8	21.0	15.8	5.3	10.5	15.8	—	105.4
Others	—	16.7	—	—	16.7	33.3	—	—	33.3	150.0

Source: Sample Survey 1981.

Table 29   Housing density of immigrant labour force in Kuwait — per person per room (%)

Person in one room Nationality	less than 1	1-	2-	3-	4-	5-	6-	7 and more	Average
Palestinians and Jordanians	4.7	29.0	36.3	18.6	8.1	1.8	1.0	0.5	2.6
Arabs from the Arabian Gulf	12.0	36.0	12.0	8.0	4.1	8.0	—	—	2.1
Egyptians	7.6	55.5	29.7	4.4	2.0	0.4	0.4	—	1.9
Other Arabs	9.8	42.1	29.9	9.4	5.8	0.4	0.4	0.4	2.2
Indians	17.3	63.5	19.2	—	—	—	—	—	1.5
Pakistanis	4.0	60.0	20.0	12.0	4.0	—	—	—	2.02
Other Asians	4.5	40.9	27.3	9.1	9.1	—	—	—	2.5
Others	71.4	19.0	4.8	4.8	—	—	:	—	0.93

Source: Sample Survey 1981.

Table 30   Length of stay in Kuwait

	%
less than one year	1.6
1-	21.9
3-	25.0
5-	20.3
7-	17.2
9 years and more	10.9
Not specified	3.2
Total	100.0

Source: Sample Survey 1983.

Table 31   Monthly income of the heads of immigrant families in Kuwait

KD	%
less than 100	4.7
100-	32.8
200-	32.8
300-	9.4
400-	4.7
500 and more	14.1
Not specified	1.6
Total	100.0

Source: Sample Survey 1983.

Table 32   Educational standards of immigrant heads of families

	%
Illiterate	3.1
Read and write	7.8
Primary	9.4
Intermediate	4.7
Secondary	23.4
Technical	12.5
University	37.5
Not specified	1.6
Total	100.0

Source: Sample Survey 1983.

Table 33   Occupation of the head of the family in Kuwait and in Egypt

Occupation	% in Kuwait	% in Egypt
Professional and technical	43.8	37.5
Administrative and managerial	1.6	7.8
Clerical	34.4	12.5
Agriculture and fishermen	1.6	6.3
Production and labourers	12.5	15.6
Others	6.3	20.3
Total	100.0	100.0

Source: Sample Survey 1983.

Table 34   Way of getting employment in Kuwait

	%
By himself	45.3
Relative in Kuwait	50.0
Job offer	3.1
Unspecified	1.6
Total	100.0

Source: Sample Survey 1983.

Table 35   Number of visits to country of origin paid by immigrant heads of families: average per year

Number of visits	%
More than once	9.4
One time	64.1
Once in two years	7.8
Once in three years	3.1
Paid no visit	12.5
Not specified	3.1
Total	100.0

Source: Sample Survey 1983.

Table 36   Occupation in Egypt of heads of immigrant families by age group

Age Group	Technical and scientific	Administrative and managerial	Clerical	Service	Agriculture and fishermen	Production and labourers	Unemployed
less than 20	–	–	–	–	–	–	14.3
20-	4.2	–	–	–	–	–	14.3
25-	16.7	40.0	37.5	33.3	25.0	30.0	28.6
30-	20.8	20.0	37.5	16.7	–	30.0	14.3
35-	20.8	40.0	12.5	33.3	50.0	30.0	14.3
40-	12.5	–	12.5	16.7	25.0	–	14.3
45-	16.7	–	–	–	–	–	–
50-	4.2	–	–	–	–	–	–
55 and over	4.2	–	–	–	–	10.0	–
Total							

Source: Sample Survey 1983.

INDEX

The following abbreviations have been used:

IW for immigrant workers
K for Kuwait